PRAISE FOR *THE SING SING FILES*

"I hope this book, which I stayed up all night reading, captures the hearts and minds of all of us. *The Sing Sing Files* illustrates on a deeply personal level what happens to real people, to their families, and to the trust in our core systems when people are sent to prison, often for decades, for crimes they didn't commit. We all play a role in allowing these miscarriages of justice to continue unless we collectively commit to seeing the flaws in our justice system and commit to rectifying them."

—Karol Mason, president of John Jay College of Criminal Justice

"Twenty years, hundreds of visits to prison, thousands of hours investigating to fight for a few men's freedom. Dan Slepian's uncommon determination, willingness to believe, and refusal to look away leap from these spellbinding pages. . . . I am grateful to Slepian for bearing witness, but I am also shocked and enraged by the story he tells."

—Nicholas Turner, president and director of the Vera Institute of Justice

"Dan Slepian has written a book that is as informative as it is enraging. In these gripping case studies of innocent men wrongfully convicted, you learn how and why the truth often does not prevail in the American justice system. You also get a glimpse of the strength of the human spirit and of heroic efforts to right these wrongs. The stories are inspiring and so is the author."

—Rachel Elise Barkow, author of *Prisoners of Politics* and professor at New York University School of Law

"Slepian's a master storyteller with a passion for his subject. This is a page-turner with stories that will open your mind and heart and might even change your life the way they changed his."

—John F. Hollway, executive director of the Quattrone Center for the Fair Administration of Justice at the University of Pennsylvania Carey Law School

"While recounting his heroic efforts to free six wrongfully convicted men, Dan Slepian uncovers the tremendous obstacles to truth and justice that plague our criminal legal system. He shows that the problems are both systemic and personal, as institutions and actors protect their own reputations rather than fix the egregious mistakes and wrongdoings that have ruined the lives of countless people and their families. *The Sing Sing Files* should inspire readers to create a new generation of leaders who will genuinely pursue justice."

—Marc Howard, director of the Prisons and Justice Initiative at Georgetown University

THE SING SING FILES

One Journalist, Six Innocent Men,
and a Twenty-Year Fight for Justice

DAN SLEPIAN

CELADON BOOKS C **NEW YORK**

www.celadonbooks.com

Designed by Jonathan Bennett

Library of Congress Cataloging-in-Publication Data

Names: Slepian, Dan, author.
Title: The Sing Sing files : one journalist, six innocent men, and a twenty-year fight for justice / Dan Slepian.
Description: First edition. | New York : Celadon Books, 2024. | Includes bibliographical references and index.
Identifiers: LCCN 2024003682 | ISBN 9781250897701 (hardcover) | ISBN 9781250897718 (ebook)
Subjects: LCSH: False imprisonment—New York (State) | Judicial error—New York (State) | Criminal justice, Administration of—New York (State) | Slepian, Dan.
Classification: LCC HV9956.N5 S547 2024 | DDC 364.152/309747—dc23/eng/20240404
LC record available at https://lccn.loc.gov/2024003682

Our books may be purchased in bulk for promotional, educational, or business use. Please contact your local bookseller or the Macmillan Corporate and Premium Sales Department at 1-800-221-7945, extension 5442, or by email at MacmillanSpecialMarkets@macmillan.com.

First Edition: 2024

10 9 8 7 6 5 4 3 2 1

To Jocelyn and Casey, the pillars of my life

CONTENTS

THE SING SING FILES

INTRODUCTION   JJ

ON THANKSGIVING DAY IN 2002, I spent the morning at Green Haven
Correctional Facility, a maximum-security prison a couple of hours north of
Manhattan, filming a story for NBC's *Dateline* about two incarcerated men[1]
who insisted they'd been wrongfully convicted of murder. I had spent a lot of
time around cops and courts, but wrongful convictions and false imprisonments were not things I knew much about when I walked into Green Haven's
dreary lobby that morning and saw a woman holding the hands of two little
boys who were staring in my direction.

"You're Dan, right?" said the woman, who introduced herself as Maria
Velazquez. "My son, Jon-Adrian—we call him JJ—is locked up here. He was
convicted of murder but he's innocent." She told me that JJ had heard I was
coming that day, and she'd told him she'd do her best to speak with me. I could
feel her pain and desperation.

"Can you help us?" Maria asked.

I looked at her and then at the two boys, whom she introduced to me as
JJ's sons: Jacob, age five, and Jon Jr., age eight. They were polite but quiet. It
seemed like it had already been a long, hard day for them—and it seemed like
they'd already had too many long, hard days.

Jon Jr. was on Maria's right side. Jacob, the littler one, was holding her left
hand. He barely came up to her waist. He stared up at me with huge, confused
eyes. He didn't say a word, but I swear he was asking me: *Who are you? Why am
I here? What's going on? How can I make it stop?*

My first thought was that, regardless of their dad's guilt or innocence, these
two little guys should have been home, running around with their cousins—
not standing in the harsh fluorescent lighting of a prison lobby.

Their grandmother told me that two years earlier, in 2000, a jury had convicted her son, JJ Velazquez, of murdering a former New York City police officer and he had been sentenced to twenty-five years to life. She insisted her only child was an innocent man.

Frankly, I doubted it. I was there investigating the claims of two other men who insisted they were innocent, and I still didn't know if they were telling the truth. What were the odds that another wrongfully convicted person would be in the same part of the same prison?

I told Maria that I couldn't make any promises, but I would read about her son's case when I could, making sure to add that it would probably not happen anytime soon. Even so, she seemed relieved. She said that for years she'd tried and failed to get anyone to listen to her.

I wasn't a father myself yet, but as I drove home, something haunted me about those weary kids in that prison lobby. I couldn't get Jacob's sad, serious eyes out of my mind. Soon enough, I wouldn't be able to get his dad's voice out of my head either.

Looking back on meeting those boys and their grandmother that Thanksgiving morning, it would have been impossible to imagine the impact those few minutes would have on my life, both professionally and personally, and the way in which my relationship with JJ would come to touch countless other lives as well. It marked the beginning of an odyssey that's still ongoing and that continues to reshape my perception of how justice functions in this country—or doesn't—and caused me to reconsider how I function as a journalist and as a human being.

This book's title refers to the prison officially known as Sing Sing Correctional Facility in Ossining, New York, the notorious maximum-security prison where JJ would spend most of the twenty-three years, seven months, and eight days of his wrongful incarceration, and where over two decades I would visit him more than two hundred times. The title also refers to how I came to investigate and produce *Dateline* reports not only about JJ but also about five other innocent men who crossed paths with him and who were also doing someone else's time. Their names are David Lemus, Olmedo Hidalgo, Eric Glisson, Johnny Hincapie, and Richard Rosario.

Over the years, as my basement has gradually grown full of boxes with their legal paperwork, I've filmed more than a thousand hours of interviews and footage connected to these men and their cases, my camera a diary of each of my investigations into their claims of innocence and the consequences of their incarceration. As a result, I've amassed a vast digital archive of video and audio—a trove that allows me to present conversations and scenes in the pages that follow with precise detail; nothing is reconstructed or embellished.

In my career as a producer for NBC News I have witnessed the American criminal justice system from every perspective. I've been embedded with detectives, prosecutors, and defense attorneys and followed them and their cases for months, sometimes years. I've interviewed countless murderers, judges, and jurors. I've gotten to know many victims of crime and have come to understand the devastating impact it has on them and their families. I've spent several hundred days inside prisons across the United States with the wardens who run them, with convicted killers sentenced to death, and with the corrections officers who walk those dangerous tiers every day, hoping to go home unharmed. And I've toured prisons in other countries. I even slept in a cell for two nights in Louisiana's Angola prison, a former slave plantation, with *NBC Nightly News* and *Dateline* anchor Lester Holt for a program about mass incarceration. And I conceived and produced the first-ever televised town hall from a maximum-security prison, Sing Sing, which was broadcast on MSNBC and moderated by Lester.

Proximity has taught me one overwhelming truth: we have an undeniable crisis on our hands. There are roughly two million Americans locked up, more than in any other country,[2] and our recidivism rates lead the world. I've seen for myself the cruel reality of how people and families have been ravaged by the system meant to protect them. I've come to see the inhumanity and irrationality of that system, and how its worst aspects are revealed by the way it handles wrongful convictions.

No one knows how many innocent people are in prison, but given the statistical likelihood of error, the number is staggering. Barry Scheck, cofounder of the Innocence Project, told me that he believes the most accurate studies estimate the error rate of convictions at about 5 percent, which would mean that as you're reading this, a hundred thousand people could be locked away in prison cells for crimes they did not commit. Other experts I've spoken with told me they believe the number could be as high as two hundred thousand. And yet, only about thirty-five hundred people have been exonerated in the past *thirty* years. Why? The system, as I have discovered, isn't built to get people out. It's built to keep them in—even when, as I will illustrate, there is clear evidence that they don't belong there.

In the course of my twenty years of doing this work, I've personally heard from more than a thousand people who claim that they were stolen without cause from their lives and families. I've read hundreds of thousands of pages of transcripts, police reports, and court motions, often hunched over my desk or swiping through pages of documents on my iPad late at night. And what I've concluded is that I can no longer accept the worn cliché that justice is blind.

Over time, what I learned is that there are myriad ways in which the system seems designed to easily imprison the innocent, and then keep them locked up despite clear evidence proving they're not guilty of the crime for which they were convicted. This work has given me a deep understanding of what false imprisonment means not only for the individuals who are wrongly removed from society but also for their parents, partners, and children. As tragic as these injustices are for innocent people in prison, they have a cascading generational impact on those around them and on society that is hard to measure.

My experience tells me that even when some prosecutors are presented with irrefutable proof of innocence, the default is resistance as opposed to curiosity or concern. All too often, an assistant district attorney will remain deliberately indifferent, willfully ignore facts, and deny reality. Year after year, decade after decade, wrongfully convicted people wither away behind bars.

Racism and corruption are part of it, absolutely. But I've come to understand other insidious ways in which wrongful convictions happen—whether through eyewitness misidentification, a false confession, prosecutorial misconduct, or bad lawyering. The problem is an epidemic. It's why I can barely manage to sleep five hours a night. The stakes are too high. The injustice is too great.

Investigating a claim of innocence is slow and beyond onerous. That's one reason the news media doesn't report on the full scope of the problem. These stories are expensive to do, are difficult to report, and can literally take decades. For that reason, diving into these cases, trying to find the truth, has become for the most part my "extracurricular" work, while my real job as a *Dateline* producer has been to produce true-crime murder-mystery sagas, special hours with Lester Holt, and hidden-camera investigations.

Bryan Stevenson's powerful, groundbreaking book *Just Mercy* is perhaps the most well-known chronicle of wrongful conviction. The heart of that book is about a case in Alabama. What I find astonishing, even after all these years, is that each of the cases you'll read about in this book happened in what is supposedly the bastion of progressivism, New York City.

I'll tell you about how JJ Velazquez and five other men were sucked into the vortex of a corrupt criminal justice system. I will connect the dots to show that guardians of the system either knew these men were innocent or simply didn't care, and in some cases angled to keep them in prison anyway—for decades.

As JJ and the other men fought for their freedom, I saw careers upended, relationships destroyed, and my own faith tested. To this day there has been no full accounting of what happened to these innocent men, and no reckoning with those who did this to them. The system that perpetrated this unnecessary suffering and brutal injustice and the prosecutors and police who were part of it have not been made to answer for the harm that was done.

My hope is that this book will help change that, providing important lessons for reporters, prosecutors, defense attorneys, detectives, judges, and jurors—and ultimately for anyone interested in living in a just society.

1   *DATELINE*

LIKE SO MANY OF us, I was raised to believe that the people who took oaths to uphold the law fairly and impartially always made sure that the bad guys, and certainly only the bad guys, wound up behind bars. Even if the system did get it wrong sometimes, I trusted there were so many checks and balances—prosecutors, defense attorneys, judges, juries, appeals—that someone staying in prison for a long time for something they didn't do was either highly unlikely or extraordinarily rare.

Early in my career as a producer for *Dateline*, my experiences only reinforced that view. I'd gotten to know and worked closely with some of the best of law enforcement, producing many hours of TV that focused on the legal system when it worked just the way it should.

In the early 2000s, I was granted rare access to film Las Vegas homicide detectives as they investigated murders in real time for a *Dateline* series I created and produced, aptly named Vegas Homicide. It was my first immersive experience with law enforcement, and it helped me understand what these brave officers were up against: from breaking devastating news that someone's loved one had been murdered to working around the clock to figure out who was responsible.

I talked my way into getting permission for this project by offering what, at the time, was a novel approach. I got hold of an early handheld camera—this was before the digital era—and pitched Las Vegas police brass that in an effort to be as unobtrusive as possible during an unfolding investigation, it would just be me riding along with their detectives. My small footprint meant there would be no camerapeople and no audio engineer running around with headphones and a long stick-boom microphone. I would be serving as the producer, reporter, cameraperson, and audio engineer all in one. While I was the first producer at *Dateline* to do this, I'd had a camera in my hand since I was big enough to hold one—which, I suppose, is how my road to *Dateline* began.

I grew up in the suburbs of New York and always wanted to work in TV news, specifically at NBC, which was the network of choice in my home. After school, I'd sit at the kitchen island as my mom made dinner, watching *The Phil Donahue Show*, followed by WNBC's local news program *Live at Five* with Sue Simmons and Tony Guida on a thirteen-inch TV above the refrigerator. The news anchors were A-list celebrities in my eyes.

In 1990, during my junior year at SUNY Stony Brook, I eagerly applied for a summer internship with WNBC, but I was rejected. Twice.

Instead, I got an internship at a good-government group across from city hall called Common Cause. The internship was intensely boring. I spent most of my time making copies in a poorly lit hallway. The most exciting part of my day was eating my lunch, people-watching, and soaking up the sunshine before returning to my lonely copier cave.

One day I saw a throng of reporters rushing into city hall looking excited. I was curious, so I followed them in. Turned out there was a press conference going on, and as an aspiring journalist, I thought I'd check it out.

A security guard at the door said, "Who are you with?"

"Independent media!" I said, proud of my spontaneous fabrication.

To my surprise, he waved me through.

Before I knew it, I was sitting in the back of what's called the "blue room," waiting for the press conference to begin, with my brown-bag lunch in my lap. And then in walked Mayor David Dinkins.

Cool! I thought. He was the first famous person I'd ever seen in the flesh.

Seconds later, I saw my second famous person: Tony fucking Guida, sitting right there in the front row. With his snow-white hair, he looked just like he did on *Live at Five*. After the news conference concluded, I stationed myself outside city hall, watching everyone as they streamed out. And there he was, Tony Guida.

I went up to him and said, no doubt with the energy of a puppy off the leash, "Mr. Guida! My name is Dan Slepian! I watch you all the time! I applied to be an intern at WNBC, but I got rejected. I'll do anything. I'll get you coffee, whatever you want."

He gazed at me for a moment. Here I was, this painfully earnest nineteen-year-old vibrating with enthusiasm and hope. And then he reached into his shirt pocket, took out a napkin, and scribbled a number on it. He handed it to me with three words: "Call Mike Callahan." Tony probably thought nothing of it, but those few seconds of kindness would forever change my professional trajectory and my life.

The very next day I dialed the number Tony had given me and spoke with Mike Callahan, the chain-smoking managing editor at WNBC. Excitement brimming in my voice, I said, "I met Tony Guida! He said to call you because I'd love to be an intern, and I—"

He cut me off and said, "Come on in."

And so the next day I found myself at the WNBC office in iconic 30 Rockefeller Plaza. Callahan wasted no time and said, "You want to be an intern? Help out the assignment editors on the desk." Simple as that. I never went back to Common Cause. In fact, I've stayed in that very building more than thirty years now.

The NBC internship coordinator would see me and say, "Who are you?"

"An intern!" I'd confidently reply.

"No, you have to be part of the program," she'd respond.

"Mike said I could come in."

"That's not the way it works," she'd say.

We would have that conversation on a few occasions. As many times as she tried to get rid of me, I just kept coming in every day, pulling faxes, answering phones, and cheerfully fetching sugar for assignment editor Harry Rittenberg's SlimFast. I was like the guy from *Office Space* who didn't have a job and just kept showing up. I'd cross paths with that internship director in the hallways for years, and she'd always have a silent stare like, *You're still here?*

That unorthodox "internship" eventually paved the way for me to be accepted into the NBC Page Program, a highly competitive opportunity for college graduates looking to get into the TV business. Among my responsibilities was giving tours of the studios and seating audiences for shows like *Late Night with David Letterman* and *Saturday Night Live*.

My first "real" job was working for the man I grew up watching after school every day. The OG, the original, pre-Oprah daytime talk show host, Phil Donahue. For the kids who don't know his name: he invented running around a studio audience holding a microphone in random people's faces, and he totally revolutionized television. When *Donahue* went off the air in 1996, I started working at *Dateline*, my dream job, and never left.

Dateline, NBC's longest-running prime-time series, has been on the air for more than thirty years and has become part of mainstream American culture. When I began there, the show was anchored by Stone Phillips and Jane Pauley, and aired two nights per week. Within a couple of years, under the leadership of executive producer Neal Shapiro, it was on as many as five nights per week.

Back then, the show was broken into several segments covering various topics, from celebrity profiles to undercover investigations to breaking news reports. Producing stories during that time was like drinking from several fire hoses at once.

My first role at *Dateline* was as what's called a booker, meaning it was my job to convince people embroiled in the biggest breaking stories of the day to talk exclusively to *Dateline*. About fifteen young staffers, mostly news nerds, were told to keep an overnight bag under our desks at work, because you never knew when news would break and you'd be headed to the airport. When the Columbine shooting happened, I was off to Colorado with Stone Phillips. When Waco was burning, I headed to Texas. When JFK Jr.'s plane went down, I was on the next flight to Martha's Vineyard.

A few years later, *Dateline* began to focus on murder mysteries, launching a new era as "the true-crime original," for its captivating yarns with twists and turns that keep viewers on the edge of their seats.

By September 10, 2001, I was thirty-one and had been working for *Dateline* for five years. I had been filming with the Vegas detectives that Monday and happened to take the last flight back from Las Vegas to New York City, where I lived at the time. I landed at about one in the morning on 9/11, and headed home to my wife, Jocelyn. Hours later, when the first plane struck the World Trade Center, I grabbed my camera, headed downtown to St. Vincent's

Hospital, and began interviewing people who were searching for their missing family members.

Looking up Seventh Avenue, I could see police cars and fire engines driving at top speed toward the bottom of the island, and I watched in awe as these men and women in uniform rushed to those buildings. In that moment, more than any other—and I'd spent a lot of time with police officers and been impressed by what they did—I thought, *These are men and women who have different blood than I do.* I'd never, not in a million years, rush into a building in flames unless my daughter was inside it. *The strength that takes, to be like them,* I thought. I'll never forget it. My heart flooded with gratitude.

The cops of the NYPD were the heroes of America and the rock stars of the city, and I wanted to embed with them much as I had in Las Vegas. So I contacted Michael O'Looney, an unusually generous deputy commissioner of public information for the NYPD, and set up a meeting to pitch my idea. About a month later I got the green light and was told I'd be following detectives in the Bronx.

So, on a sunny morning in April 2002, I arrived at the headquarters of the Bronx Homicide Task Force, camera in hand, eager and—looking back—unbelievably naive.

Located on Simpson Street in the South Bronx, the wood-paneled building immortalized in the Paul Newman movie *Fort Apache, the Bronx* two decades earlier had the faded glamour of a palace in the middle of Baghdad. I walked up a large curved staircase to the second floor, where I saw a thin gold plate that said BRONX HOMICIDE fastened to a wood door. Walking into that office was like walking back in time. There was flypaper hanging from the ceilings and the sound of officers clicking away at typewriters, using carbon paper to write police reports. The place reeked of cigarettes, even though that was the year Mayor Michael Bloomberg had outlawed indoor smoking.

I was taken to see Lieutenant Sean O'Toole, the unit's boss, and he introduced me to the two detectives the NYPD had chosen for me to follow: a legendary Bronx homicide detective named Bobby Addolorato and his equally formidable partner, John Schwartz. They were friendly, kind of, but I quickly got the sense they were not exactly thrilled with having a *Dateline* producer tagging along after them. They made it clear that they didn't particularly want to be on TV and saw my presence as more of an order than an opportunity. But they did as they were told—they were nothing if not dutiful—and eventually they got used to me and my camera.

Bobby, a son of the Bronx, had the swagger of a man who knew he was where he belonged, doing the work he was meant to do. He told me that from a young age, his parents taught him and his brother that honest public service was the measure of success, and that the Addolorato brothers always had their heart set on the action-packed version of public service promised by police work. And the main lesson his father, a city sanitation worker, stressed for this exciting way of fighting for those who can't fight for themselves? "Stay true." The cornerstone of Bobby's upbringing and career had been the quaint notion that the truth will win out, that facts are king.

Bobby's partner, John Schwartz, was also part of a police family. John's father, uncle, brother, and brother-in-law were all in the NYPD. John took and passed the police exam when he was still a teenager, and he joined the family business at his first chance, when he turned twenty. Linebacker-sized, his hair snow-white, John looked older than his years and was all business.

It didn't take me long to learn that being a detective in NYC was much different than it was in Vegas. The Vegas cops, for starters, had way more institutional support. They had department-issued cellphones. New York cops had to use their own cellphones, and there was no policy of reimbursing them for the hundreds of calls made during an investigation. Vegas detectives each had their own department-issued car. In the Bronx, detectives shared old junkers that in some cases were so beat up they needed a milk crate to support the seats. Bobby and John didn't even have official email addresses. They had to print their own business cards to hand out when asking people to contact them with tips.

As for their hours, you'd need an MBA to understand how the department is organized, but basically it works like this: All detectives are assigned to one of four "teams," lettered from A to D. For each team, there is a four-day rotation of shifts, starting at 4:00 p.m. on the first day. Detectives work 4:00 p.m. to 1:00 a.m., then 4:00 p.m. to 1:00 a.m. again the next day. Then comes the "turnaround." The next two days, their shifts begin at 8:00 a.m., so if it takes them an hour to get home to bed, on the first day of the turnaround that leaves time for only about four hours of sleep at most before they have to be back at the precinct. Homicide cops never really get much rest—it's part of the job—but this ABCD system ensured it. Even veteran detectives worked this schedule. And so did I.

Despite it all, this was Bobby Addolorato's dream job. He was happy as long as he had his coffee, the good coffee—French vanilla from the automatic machine at the Texaco station on 182nd Street.

At age forty-one, Bobby was at the top of his game. He would soon be promoted to the highest rank for a detective, first grade, earned by roughly three hundred of more than five thousand detectives in the NYPD who carry the coveted gold shield, an achievement his partner, John, had recently earned. Bobby loved working at Bronx Homicide, where he could parachute as needed into fresh homicides, and the boss was a tolerant lieutenant who would let him blast his Bruce Springsteen CDs in the squad room.

By the time I met him, Bobby had been on the job for eighteen years and had made around fifteen hundred arrests. He'd taken down some of the most violent killers the city had ever seen. He'd walked countless miles through dangerous back alleys, always trying to figure out the same things: *What happened? Who did it? How? Where are they and when can I pick them up?*

I worked Bobby and John's hours, ate at their hangouts, and saw the grisly crime scenes they worked, so we spent a lot of time together. Bobby and I soon formed a special bond. Perhaps that's why he decided to tell me about something that had nothing to do with the idea I had pitched. It was about two weeks into our project.

"You see some terrible things," I said to Bobby. "You must bring this job home."

"You know, I really don't," he told me. Then he paused. "Except this one case. It keeps me up at night."

What happened in that case, Bobby explained, was that two men were serving twenty-five years to life for a 1990 murder he believed they didn't commit.

"How do you know they didn't do it?" I asked.

"Because," he said, "I know who the real killers are."

2   THE PALLADIUM

SITTING IN THE BACKSEAT of an unmarked police car as detectives Bobby Addolorato and John Schwartz raced to the scene of a murder, sirens blaring, driving a thousand miles an hour under the elevated trains in the Bronx, I felt like I was in a scene from the 1970s action thriller *The French Connection*. My adrenaline was pumping. This was the kind of ride that journalists like me dream of, in the heart of the action.

But my mind and focus were elsewhere. I couldn't stop thinking about what Bobby had recently told me: that he believed two innocent men named David Lemus and Olmedo Hidalgo were languishing in prison for the 1990 Thanksgiving night murder of a bouncer at the Palladium nightclub in Manhattan. Bobby said he was convinced Lemus and Hidalgo were innocent because he believed that the guys who had done it were two gang members from the Bronx whom he'd investigated and arrested for other murders, Thomas "Spanky" Morales and Joey Pillot. In the weeks after we met, I peppered Bobby with questions. It was a story I wanted to know more about, and it was pulling me in.

To help me understand why he thought Spanky and Joey were guilty and Lemus and Hidalgo were innocent of the Palladium murder, Bobby said he had to take me back to his early years on the job. At the time he graduated from the police academy, in 1985, crime was surging in New York at unprecedented levels. While tabloids portray the city today as more dangerous than it's ever been, that's objectively not true, not by a long shot. In 1990, when Bobby was a young cop, New York's murder rate was the highest in the city's history. That year there were 2,245 murders—and 100,280 robberies.[1] By contrast, in 2022 there were 438 murders, down from 488 in 2020—and 17,411 robberies.[2]

One of the biggest stories back then had happened in 1989—the rape of a jogger in Central Park. Five teenagers were arrested and paraded in front of dozens of rolling cameras. The "Central Park Five"—or the "Exonerated Five," as they became known after their convictions were vacated in 2002—were described as a group of "wilding teens" who brutally raped a woman and left her for dead. Donald Trump ran an ad in *Newsday* calling for their execution, headlined: "Bring Back the Death Penalty! Bring Back Our Police!"

A year later came another horrible act of violence: the random and senseless murder of a twenty-two-year-old tourist from Utah named Brian Watkins, who was visiting New York with his family over Labor Day weekend to attend the US Open tennis championship. As they were heading out to dinner, the family was mugged by a group of teenagers on a Midtown subway platform. Brian was stabbed to death, and the city exploded. Enough was enough. The *New York Post* ran a full-front-page cover pleading with then-mayor David Dinkins: "Dave, Do Something!" and articles with headlines like "New York Streets Are Awash in Blood!"

Within two days, detectives had their suspects in the subway stabbing, saying that they'd all confessed on videotape. Like the Central Park Five, this alleged "wolf pack" of seven teenagers were paraded in front of the city's news media as they piled into a police van. Despite only one of them having a knife, all would be convicted of murder and sentenced to twenty-five years to life. Years later, I would learn that one of those teenagers was innocent and would be robbed of the next quarter century of his life.

Then, on Thanksgiving night 1990, just two months after the subway stabbing, there was a high-profile shooting at the Palladium, an enormous nightclub in the East Village, Manhattan's scruffy bohemian enclave. Two hotheads were ejected and began arguing with the bouncers. They then walked down the street to get their guns from the trunk of their car, came back with a few friends, and started shooting right there on Fourteenth Street, killing Markus Peterson, a Palladium bouncer.

Bobby was up in the Bronx at the time and knew nothing about it. "I had never heard about the Palladium murder in 1990 when it actually happened," Bobby said. "Not only did Manhattan feel like a different country, but I had my hands full back then."

Bobby was a detective assigned to the 40th Precinct, or the "4-0," in the

South Bronx. It was known as "the baddest station in the nation," because at the time, Bobby's precinct was among the most violent in America.

According to census records, it was the single poorest precinct in New York, one of the most dangerous, drug-infested places to live in the whole country. The median income of the South Bronx in 1991, according to the *New York Times*, was $7,600,[3] just over $17,000 when adjusted for inflation.[4]

Bobby and his fellow officers were investigating a never-ending stream of killings, rapes, and shootings. He would come to learn that much of the violence was committed by the C&C gang, as it was known, led by George "Cal" Calderon and Angel Padilla, Calderon's cousin, whose nickname was "Cuson."

Bobby explained to me that in the early 1990s he was the detective assigned to take down the C&C gang, and he would come to understand the inner workings and brutal crimes of C&C better than some of its members. On an organizational chart Bobby showed me of the gang, George Calderon was the Bronx's John Gotti, the kingpin running the business and orchestrating the violence, but Bobby could rattle off the name of every last henchman like they were relatives.

As Bobby described the operation for me, he seemed almost impressed by how diabolically clever the whole thing was.

"Rather than sell drugs, C&C would rent out corners in the neighborhood to various dealers. Each corner in the neighborhood was leased by different dealers selling crack and heroin. In exchange, C&C would provide security from competition and from other criminals. For every dollar sold, C&C would get a cut, and never had to touch the drugs."

Bobby explained that George Calderon and Angel "Cuson" Padilla were both mass murderers and shrewd businessmen.

"Calderon and Cuson had the cruelest, most sadistic enforcers in the city on their payroll. I mean, *bad dudes*. They dressed in black and carried guns as they patrolled the streets and collected rent, so ruthless that even the hardest drug dealers found them scary."

The seven square blocks C&C owned were the Walmart of the trade, supplying drugs to much of the East Coast, and from this humble location C&C regularly netted $400,000 a month—at least. Calderon demanded payment a week in advance, and he had about seventy or eighty dealers renting space at any given time.

One day Bobby drove me to a block C&C once controlled, pulled his cruiser into a parking spot, and pointed up at the roof.

"George Calderon, wearing a long fur coat, would stand up there and fling handfuls of bills down onto the street." He mimicked flinging money down like rain. "He'd yell down, 'Go home and feed your kids and tell them Uncle Georgie loves them!' And men, women, and children would pocket as much of the money as they could as they shouted back, 'Calderon, we love you!'"

To the families who lived there, Calderon provided hope. And if anyone ever needed a savior, it was the residents of this part of the world. He fed them, clothed them, and protected them. He owned the neighborhood.

What made it all work so efficiently, Bobby explained, were "the rules" and their strict enforcement. Calderon considered himself the sheriff of these streets. Some of the rules were obvious: pay your weekly rent to the security force. Others were more idiosyncratic: no drug sales while children walked to and from school.

"In his own twisted way, Calderon saw himself as ethical," Bobby told me with a laugh. A first violation of those "rules" resulted in a warning that came in the form of a fairly simple beating, perhaps a black eye and a fat lip, and a minimum fine of $500.

Second violation: the dealer who broke the rules got a "chicken leg," meaning he'd be shot in the kneecap and forced to hop around like a chicken.

If there was a third infraction, the penalty was death. "So, you're dead, no question," Bobby said. "The only question was how grisly it would be, like they might just pull your teeth out with a wrench before they did it, or they'd get more creative."

In the basement of C&C's headquarters at 550 East 139th Street, scores of victims were pistol-whipped, hacksawed, and electrocuted. I was riveted by Bobby's stories about atrocities that had happened only miles from my own apartment.

Bobby explained that as a young patrol officer, he would sit in his crappy undercover police car with springs from the seat poking into his back as he watched Calderon drive through the neighborhood in his Rolls-Royce like he owned the place. Bobby vowed to take the neighborhood away from C&C. He hated to think that a whole generation of children would grow up thinking this was the way life was. What irked him most was Calderon's unabashed arrogance, as if daring Bobby to challenge him.

He told me one story that even he admitted sounded like it came from Hollywood. One day he was sitting in his cruiser on a stakeout when Calderon came up from behind and knocked on his window.

Bobby rolled it down.

"Just so you know, I'm in charge here," Calderon informed the young cop.

"There's a new sheriff in town," Bobby replied.

When I first met Bobby, one of the first things he said to me was, "All you have in this life is your word. I stand by everything I say and do." It was a reputation he maintained with both colleagues and crooks. He'd tell you how he saw it, and he always kept his promises.

This philosophy had served Bobby well and made him particularly gifted at cultivating informants. One of the most valuable sources was Benny Rodriguez, a member of the C&C gang and Calderon's cousin, driver, and bodyguard. Benny was a real trip—a former crackhead and stickup artist who cruised the city streets in a Cutlass.

In 1992, Benny had a falling-out with the gang after he testified in a murder case against a fellow C&C guy. This betrayal led Bobby to compare Benny to Fredo from *The Godfather*.

Somehow Benny managed to escape with his life, although a gang member had put a gun in his mouth and broken his arm. The experience spurred Benny to cut a deal, confessing to his own gun and drug charges in exchange for becoming an informant and a valuable source of information for Bobby to learn about the inner workings of C&C and the crimes members of the gang committed.

"He's giving up everybody at this point," Bobby said. "He was trying not to get killed. He wanted to go into witness protection."

Benny was being kept hidden in a hotel in Queens by the NYPD, which is where Bobby went to speak with him. Among the many crimes that Benny told Bobby about in that hotel room was a murder that Benny said he'd witnessed two years earlier, in 1990, at the Palladium nightclub in Manhattan on Thanksgiving night. Bobby had never heard about it.

Bobby recounted for me what Benny told him, and I would later interview Benny myself on camera, twelve years after the Palladium murder, standing on the street outside where it all happened.

Benny said that on Thanksgiving night in 1990, the C&C crew was ready for some downtime. After a huge meal at the home of the boss's sister, the C&C enforcers put on their leather jackets and silk shirts, looking forward to salsa dancing and picking up women at the Palladium. Featuring a dozen Latin bands, the club would draw more than two thousand people that night.

Sluggish after too much turkey, C&C's boss, Calderon, didn't want to join his boys. So as soon as it was clear he was no longer needed by the boss, well after midnight, Benny drove to the Palladium alone, he said. While circling in his Cutlass for a parking spot by the nightclub on Fourteenth Street, Benny saw two C&C enforcers, Thomas "Spanky" Morales and Joey Pillot, outside the club.

"I'd parked my car across the street, and I was ready to go in when I saw Spanky and Joey coming out of the club. They're, like, drunk, one holding the other guy. I'm thinking, 'What the fuck is going on?' They go away. So, when I'm looking in the rearview mirror, I see them both coming back running. I saw Spanky and Joey both with guns, and then all of a sudden, I saw Spanky open fire on the bouncers."

Benny mimicked, "Bang Bang. I'm just looking at Spanky's gun going off. Joey had his gun, too. But I didn't see Joey's gun go off. There was a lotta people ducking down. And two guys fell. It was a Black guy and a white dude. Both of them hit the floor."

Benny was right. Two men were shot. The Black man was Markus Peterson, a twenty-three-year-old Palladium bouncer. His injuries were fatal. Five foot eleven, with cut muscles and broad shoulders, Markus was serious about bodybuilding and dreamed about entering national competitions. He also volunteered his time teaching weightlifting to kids at a Brooklyn recreation center near his home. The bouncer's gig was just a way to make extra money and sample Manhattan nightlife.

The white man Benny saw get shot was the Palladium's security boss, former Manhattan police officer Jeffrey Craig, age thirty, who would survive a gunshot to his leg. Turned out Craig's old precinct was the nearby 9th. His former colleagues would be the ones to handle the Palladium investigation and were hell-bent on finding the gunmen who had hurt one of their own.

Back in December 1992, after Bobby heard all this from Benny and confirmed there had been a Thanksgiving night murder two years earlier at the Palladium, Bobby brought Benny to meet with Stephen Saracco, the Manhattan assistant district attorney responsible for the Palladium case.

At the DA's office, Saracco asked Bobby to wait outside while he questioned Benny alone. "I thought it was strange," Bobby remembered. "After interviewing Benny for about a half an hour, Saracco came out, looked me straight in the eye, and said, 'You know what, kid? He's not on the money with his facts.'"

Saracco explained to Bobby that just a few weeks earlier he'd taken two other men to trial for the murder, David Lemus and Olmedo Hidalgo, and a jury had convicted them.

Saracco was confident: "We got the right guys."

So, who were David Lemus and Olmedo Hidalgo?

3   DAVID LEMUS AND OLMEDO HIDALGO

THE 1990 THANKSGIVING NIGHT murder of Markus Peterson at the Palladium nightclub touched off a citywide manhunt for his killers, and Manhattan detective Victoria Garcia of the NYPD was assigned as the lead investigator. It was her third homicide investigation.

Seven weeks later, David Lemus, a twenty-two-year-old Hispanic man with floppy dark hair, was at a courthouse for a probation violation hearing after he was caught riding in a stolen car. That's where Detective Garcia found Lemus and told him his mug shot had been picked out by witnesses to the shootings at the Palladium.

Police later claimed that, also as a result of eyewitness identifications, they had captured Lemus's accomplice, Olmedo Hidalgo, who was twenty-four. In 1992, the Manhattan DA tried Lemus and Hidalgo together, and they were convicted of second-degree murder and sentenced to twenty-five years to life.

I met Lemus and Hidalgo a decade later, in 2002, a couple of months after Bobby first told me about them. Both were housed at Green Haven Correctional Facility, a New York State maximum-security prison. That August I interviewed both men on camera as they sat at desks in a prison classroom with their legs and wrists chained. Because Hidalgo didn't speak English and I don't speak Spanish, Lemus served as an interpreter. A couple of times during the interview, when the men became emotional, I wiped away their tears because, with their hands shackled, they couldn't reach their faces on their own.

At the time of the murder, Lemus told me, he was living in the Bronx with his mother and was a part-time construction worker. He said he sometimes scored cocaine for his friends and was once caught riding in a stolen car, but that had been the extent of his legal problems.

At the time, Lemus had a steady girlfriend named Janice Catala, but he was also involved with Dolores Spencer, an older, married mother of three. Lemus said Dolores cared about fast cars and tough guys, and he wanted to impress her. When he heard a TV news report about the Palladium shooting the day after it happened, he claimed that he had done it, painting himself as avenging a woman's honor in hope that the display of machismo might impress his married lover. It was a boast he would deeply regret.

I already knew the details of the crime from reading through police reports and court transcripts. I knew that David's story didn't match up with the facts of what actually happened at the Palladium that night, but of course Dolores didn't know that and had confided in a friend about what Lemus had told her. A few weeks later, when the friend was arrested on a prostitution charge, she offered up the tidbit of information she'd learned from Dolores in exchange for leniency. And that's why detectives picked up Lemus, brought him to the 9th Precinct, and put him in a lineup.

"I didn't think that it was gonna go any further than that precinct. You know?" David told me. "I was saying to myself, 'I know I wasn't there, so they're not gonna pick me out.'"

David was wrong.

"Once the lineup was over, the detective came in the room," he said. "And I remember looking at him like, 'What's up? Can I go now?' And he was like, 'I don't know what to tell you, man.' I'm like, 'What do you mean, you don't know what to tell me?'"

It turned out that three bouncers, including Jeffrey Craig, the ex-cop who had been shot in the leg, had picked out Lemus, while three others could not make an identification. Lemus was arrested on the spot for murder. He pleaded not guilty, insisting he hadn't been at the Palladium that evening, and had an alibi: he'd been at home with his girlfriend Janice that Thanksgiving night.

Lemus made bail, and for months he continued to speak with Dolores Spencer, who he didn't know was cooperating with the authorities. They had convinced her that she had reason to fear Lemus because she was the one responsible for his arrest. Dolores agreed to let the police secretly record her phone calls with Lemus, and there were hours of them.

"Why should I be afraid of you?" she said, turning serious during one flirty exchange.

"Because you know that I know that you know," replied Lemus, who made three sounds, which prosecutors would argue to a jury referred to the Palladium shooting but which Lemus said he'd made mimicking Dolores during sex.

Later, at trial, defense attorneys lost a bid to play other portions of that tape recording for the jurors in which Lemus talked about how Dolores was afraid because her children's father would find out that they were sleeping together, and predicted that he'd receive a hefty financial settlement for being falsely accused: "My lawyer says no matter what, I'm getting at least seven digits for spending 106 days in jail for something I did not do."

Nearly a year after Lemus was arrested, detectives announced they'd found his accomplice, Olmedo Hidalgo, an undocumented immigrant from the Dominican Republic who lived in Washington Heights, a Dominican enclave in Upper Manhattan, where he worked as a clerk at his brother's bodega. Records are vague about how Hidalgo became a suspect. It almost seems that he was plucked from thin air, since he had no connection at all to the Palladium. But in late 1991 Hidalgo was arrested for carrying a gun near his home. When police ran his name, they found that an informant apparently had told police that he was one of the Palladium shooters, but for some reason he wasn't picked up for almost a year.

At their trial in November 1992, Manhattan assistant district attorney Stephen Saracco argued to the jury that Lemus and Hidalgo had acted together in ambushing the bouncers and were responsible for Markus Peterson's death. Three eyewitnesses, all bouncers, including Jeffrey Craig, the former officer who had been shot in the leg, testified that Lemus and Hidalgo were the killers.

In fact, Lemus and Hidalgo didn't know each other, and the prosecution didn't present a shred of evidence to show any connection between the two. There was no physical, forensic, or DNA evidence connecting either one to the scene—no recovered weapons, no fingerprints, no security videotape—and not a single customer reported ever seeing Lemus or Hidalgo that night.

Lemus and Hidalgo's court-appointed attorneys did not call a single witness to the stand, despite each defendant claiming to have an alibi.

Testimony from the bouncers and Lemus's bragging to Dolores were enough. On December 2, 1992, after one day of deliberation, the jury convicted both men.

The defense provided to Lemus and Hidalgo represents a much larger systemic issue: the lack of an authentic constitutional right to counsel for the indigent. Despite popular belief, "court-appointed," or public, attorneys are often not a problem in and of themselves. In fact, they are often passionate and effective advocates for the accused. The real issue is the amount of time and money required for a zealous defense and public defenders' inability to provide it, while prosecutors have an entire police agency as their investigative arm, whatever it costs. When defendants talk about an "unfair playing field," this is among the reasons.

Meanwhile, it was only a few weeks after Lemus and Hidalgo's trial had ended that a young detective from the Bronx named Bobby Addolorato brought his confidential informant Benny Rodriguez to the Manhattan DA's office to meet with prosecutor Stephen Saracco.

Bobby remembers being surprised when Saracco told him that Benny, who had always been a reliable informant, was wrong about Spanky and Joey being the gunmen. But Bobby simply figured, *Okay, maybe Benny was mistaken this time. I guess they got the right guys.*

"Hey, not a problem," Bobby said to Saracco. "You guys know the case better than me. Just doin' my job, figured I'd share what I'd heard."

Bobby walked out of that meeting and forgot about it until two years later.

By 1994, Bobby's lieutenant had taken him off regular duty and assigned him to focus strictly on building the case against George Calderon, Angel "Cuson" Padilla, and their army of hoodlums. As Bobby and his partner at the time, Ricky Burnham, started to dig in, they found that the C&C operation was even bigger and crueler than they'd imagined. By now, in addition to Bobby's informant Benny Rodriguez, they'd amassed a mountain of evidence against C&C, and they'd arrested twenty-one members of the gang, charging them with thirty-one murders and fourteen attempted murders.[1] To Bobby's disappointment, though, George Calderon was not one of those charged. He had been killed in a hit ordered by his partner in crime, Angel Padilla, his own cousin.

Bobby's investigation became so large and consequential that it grew into a federal case under the RICO (Racketeer Influenced and Corrupt Organizations) statute—the same one that around the same time took down John Gotti. As a result, Bobby began working with federal prosecutors, one of whom was Steven Cohen, an assistant United States attorney from the Southern District of New York (SDNY).

Fresh from two prestigious jobs clerking for federal judges, Steve Cohen had jumped at the chance to become an AUSA assigned to the gang task force, the first step in a career that would eventually take him to Albany as Andrew Cuomo's top deputy when Cuomo was New York's attorney general and later in the governor's office.

"In the months of 1994 after we make our arrests of the C&C crew, we start moving towards trial preparation," Cohen told me. "We're debriefing our arrestees, people who want to come in for a plea, or people who want to come into a cooperation agreement with the government."

These debriefings are called "proffer sessions" (or sometimes the US attorney's office calls them "Queen for a Day"), and they happen in the SDNY when the federal government gives people who want to cooperate an opportunity to cut a deal by admitting to every crime they've ever committed, whether the government knows about those crimes or not, and plead guilty to all of them. In exchange, the prosecutor writes a letter to the judge, who can then offer leniency. This incentivizes people charged with serious offenses to tell the truth no matter how horrible the crimes are. But if the government ever learns you've lied, even if they learn it years later, the deal is torn up and you could be facing mandatory life.

It fell to a natural talker like Cohen to be among the prosecutors who teamed up with Bobby to interrogate the arrested C&C gang members over several months to make sure that they came clean.

One of the gang members Bobby arrested during that roundup was C&C enforcer Joey Pillot, who wanted to save himself from a life sentence by testifying against his former boss. But before the feds agreed to a deal, they had to make sure Pillot would be a solid witness for the prosecution. He couldn't hide any past crimes from them.

After several days of Cohen explaining the benefits of such a deal and the consequences of rejecting it, with Bobby by his side taking notes, Pillot copped to pulling the trigger in three gang murders and plotting six others. But Cohen sensed that Pillot was still holding back. "I said to Joey, 'Whatever it is you think we will never know, that is what you need to tell us now. If we don't hear it from you, I have no doubt that we will be hearing it from your former pals. And if that happens, if we hear it from them and not from you, there'll be nothing I can do; you will spend the rest of your life in prison.'"

"You mean the Palladium murder?" Pillot said.

"Tell me about that," said Cohen without missing a beat, though he hadn't had a clue about the Palladium nightclub murder until that very second.

Pillot proceeded to describe what happened that Thanksgiving night in 1990, explaining how his fellow gang member Spanky got punched in the face by one of the bouncers, which prompted him and Spanky to retaliate.

Sitting next to Cohen, Bobby felt a chill run up his spine. He couldn't believe what he was hearing. "It was an instant flashback two years earlier to Benny," he told me. "The same story."

Just like Benny had claimed, Joey confirmed that he and Spanky had gone to their car, grabbed their guns from the trunk, and returned to the club. Both men opened fire, but Joey said his gun jammed and an unfired bullet fell to the street.

"Joey Pillot knew certain things about that crime scene that only somebody who was there would have known," Bobby said. "The ballistic evidence was .38 calibers in the doors and in the bodies. And there was one live 9-millimeter found on the floor that nobody could ever explain, except that day Joey explained it."

After Pillot's 1994 admission, Bobby and Steve Cohen started to debrief more C&C gang members and learned that several had critical information. "They told us Spanky said, 'Yeah, we lit them up. We shot the bouncer,'" Bobby remembered. "We wound up with three more witnesses on top of Joey's confession."

Bobby learned there was even more evidence, including an anonymous call to a tip hotline saying Joey and Spanky were responsible for the Palladium shooting. The caller even gave the address of the C&C headquarters in the Bronx.

Two years earlier, Bobby's informant Benny had told Stephen Saracco, the Palladium prosecutor, the same information, but Saracco insisted Lemus and Hidalgo were the guilty ones. Now, Steve Cohen, with the weight of the US attorney's office behind him, brought all of this new information back to Saracco once again. Still, Saracco stood by the convictions, but he did agree to hold a so-called 440 hearing, referring to Section 440.10(g) of the New York Code, which allows for a judge to decide whether to vacate a judgment when new evidence is discovered.

That hearing was held in April 1996 before Justice Jay Gold, the same judge who had presided over Lemus and Hidalgo's trial. Joey Pillot, who was serving time for his C&C crimes, was brought from prison to testify and swore under oath that he and Spanky were the real gunmen. Spanky, like Joey, was in federal custody as part of the C&C case. He said he would testify about what happened if prosecutors granted him immunity, but the Manhattan DA refused the offer.

On the witness stand, Pillot said something that seemed innocuous. When asked to identify whom he knew that night at the Palladium, he included a man named Richie—Richie Feliciano. Pillot said Richie was a heavyset man who tried to mediate the dispute between Spanky and the bouncers when he was kicked out. That name would become important later.

Pillot's wife also testified, saying the couple had been partying with friends at the club that night. Another C&C gang member told the court that he had heard Pillot brag about the bouncer's killing in the days afterward. Steve Cohen also testified. But Saracco wasn't having any second thoughts, at least publicly. He pointed out that when Pillot first confessed he had lied in saying that he, not Spanky, was the gunman. Pillot would later admit he was trying to protect his friend Spanky, but Saracco suggested that Pillot was just lying again, this time concocting a story to help his friends Lemus and Hidalgo, even though there was zero evidence the men knew one another.

Most of all, Saracco argued that even if the information incriminated Pillot or Spanky Morales, it did not mean that Lemus or Hidalgo was innocent.

Ultimately, Justice Gold agreed with Saracco. He described Joey Pillot as "entirely unworthy of belief" and suggested that Bobby Addolorato and Steve Cohen were unwitting dupes. There would be no new trial for Lemus and Hidalgo.

Cohen, an experienced federal prosecutor, was perplexed and troubled by the decision. Bobby was stunned: "My jaw just dropped," he said. "I mean, at that point, you want to run and bang on the judge's chamber door and say, 'Wait, you've got to hear this whole story, your honor!' I figured they'd get a new trial, and when all the evidence would come out it would be overwhelming."

Instead, Lemus and Hidalgo were sent back to prison. Bobby went back to his regular routine of catching homicides up in the Bronx. Cohen left the US attorney's office and started working for a white-shoe law firm. Still, the Palladium case continued to nag at both of them. The thought of Lemus and Hidalgo locked up year after year was a burden that both Bobby and Steve carried. But the detective and the attorney were unsure what they could do about it.

Cohen eventually came up with a plan. If the courthouse doors were locked, he figured that maybe the court of public opinion might be open, so he tried to get some media attention for the case—and succeeded. On July 25, 2000, the *New York Times* ran a front-page story headlined "Another Confessed in Killing but Two Men Remain in Prison," written by Jane Fritsch and David Rhode.

Someone who was at the Palladium that night read the *Times* story and came forward to say he had been involved with the crime and knew exactly what happened.

4   BAD COP MOVIE

IN THE FAST-PACED WORLD of prime-time television, every hour is precious real estate. My bosses at *Dateline* have the daunting task of sorting through thousands of pitches each year and selecting only a fraction of them to greenlight. By necessity, they favor stories with a clear beginning, middle, and end—like a trial with a verdict. This approach ensures a reliable production schedule and a focused budget.

But when I showed up at Bronx Homicide in 2002, I found myself immersed in something fundamentally different after detective Bobby Addolorato told me that he believed two innocent guys were in prison but no one was listening.

Even if I could prove Lemus and Hidalgo were wrongfully convicted, I knew the story would still probably be a hard sell. My bosses were wary of investigations into questionable miscarriages of justice—not because they didn't care, but because these kinds of stories often fail to gain traction with audiences. Most important, they take forever, or longer, to play out. Investigating a wrongful conviction claim defied conventional crime-and-punishment narratives. I was on something of a fishing expedition that was taking a lot of time and costing NBC money, and I still had a lot of work ahead of me before I would know if it was even worth pitching as a prime-time hour of TV. But, driven by Bobby's certainty, I became fixated on uncovering the truth about David Lemus and Olmedo Hidalgo.

When I arrived at Bronx Homicide, Bobby told me that the latest development in the case had happened a couple of years earlier, in 2000, when that *New York Times* article brought a crucial witness out of the shadows: Richie Feliciano, a Bronx gang member in prison on federal drug charges. When Feliciano got his phone time after reading the story, he made a collect call to the man who had locked him up. That was John O'Malley, an investigator with the gang crimes unit at the US attorney's office for the Southern District of New York.

Before working for the feds, John O'Malley had worked in the Bronx with the NYPD for twenty years. Bobby and John were close friends; the rare moments of downtime they had together were usually filled with drinks and rounds of golf. You couldn't find two guys who worked harder or respected each other more. Every now and then I'd tag along with Bobby and John for a beer after work and listen to them swap war stories from their early days as young officers.

John O'Malley knew more about New York's gangs than just about anyone on earth, save Bobby. And he was thorough. Preet Bharara, a former United States attorney for the Southern District of New York, wrote in his book that "light had a better chance of escaping a black hole than a fact had of escaping from John O'Malley's brain."

Like Bobby, O'Malley was a straight shooter who formed a "my word is my bond" relationship with informants and killers. Richie Feliciano, a career criminal, was one of those people. So much so that Richie called John to talk about that *Times* article. *Wait—Richie Feliciano reads the* New York Times? O'Malley thought when they got on the phone.

Feliciano told O'Malley that he had been at the Palladium that night hanging out with Joey and Spanky, and that he'd tried to calm things down between them and the bouncers. Then he said, "Those guys [Lemus and Hidalgo] in the story weren't the guys! It was Joey and Spanky."

O'Malley shared what Richie told him with his boss, assistant US attorney Nicole LaBarbara. They contacted Manhattan ADA Saracco and told him that Feliciano confirmed Spanky and Joey had been the shooters at the Palladium—the same information that the lead detective, Victoria Garcia, had gotten from the tip call just six days after the crime, the same information Saracco had heard about a decade earlier from C&C informant Benny Rodriguez and then again from Joey Pillot when he confessed on the stand.

But neither Saracco nor anyone else from the Manhattan DA's office was interested in interviewing Feliciano.

O'Malley and LaBarbara were baffled. To them, the information was bulletproof, especially because if Feliciano was lying, his cooperation agreement would be torn up and he'd be facing an automatic life sentence. Not to mention the fact that what he said matched everything the Manhattan DA's office had been told for a decade. But the Manhattan prosecutors continued to insist that the right guys were behind bars.

That doesn't necessarily mean that anyone was behaving in bad faith. People in nearly every aspect of the system often suffer from subconscious issues that contribute to wrongful convictions, like confirmation bias, racial bias, or even simple tunnel vision—rejecting information that doesn't comport with what they believe to be true.[1]

Whatever the reason, Lemus and Hidalgo remained in prison. Another two years went by with no action by prosecutors. Then, in 2002, I showed up and became laser focused on learning about every twist in the Palladium case. The more Bobby put the pieces together for me, the more I felt my blood pressure rising. It was hard to believe that a decorated cop and other respected people in law enforcement couldn't get the Manhattan DA's office to act. *Aren't all these guys on the same team?* I thought.

Looking back, I shudder to think how much I had to learn.

For me, what I was hearing was also unsettling on a personal level. The NYPD was my police force. The Manhattan district attorney was the chief law enforcement officer of my city. Could institutions so powerful and consequential do whatever they wanted with impunity? I felt compelled to push the story forward, but there was a problem: investigating Bobby's hunch about a wrongful conviction wasn't the reason I had been given permission to ride along with him. I was there to follow him and his partner as they investigated new murders, not dissect old ones where mistakes might have been made. NYPD brass weren't aware of Bobby's obsession with the Palladium case, or that he believed his Manhattan colleagues had locked up two innocent guys. But this was the story that I was fixated on.

Bobby said that before he did anything relating to the Palladium case in front of my camera, he wanted police headquarters to approve my new focus. And so did Adam Gorfain, the senior producer at *Dateline* overseeing my project. So on September 13, 2002, five months after arriving at Fort Apache, I sent a letter to NYPD deputy commissioner Mike O'Looney, thanking him for his help so far and telling him about a potential change in my plans. After some niceties, I got down to why I wanted to switch focus:

> We understand that at this point, Det. Addolorato believes that, through no fault of his colleagues in the police department or in the Manhattan DA's office, new leads have surfaced that need to be followed in what he sees as a search for the truth about what happened at the Palladium on the night of November 23, 1990. Although he has said he would very much like to be able to discuss the case publicly, he respects his chain of command and has told us he can't yet go on television until he's sure his chief and your office are on board.

No concerns were expressed by O'Looney or anyone else about my new plan, and Bobby got permission from his supervisor to discuss it with me. So I took out my camera and hit record as Bobby took a Sharpie and created a new case folder with the label PALLADIUM on it. Bobby was optimistic and excited, saying he'd follow the evidence wherever it went and for as long as it took.

I'd first arrived at Bronx Homicide for a project that had begun as a fairly routine ride-along with detectives. I would soon bear witness to a kind of justice system that I had never known existed.

Bobby had already collected some police reports, transcripts, and other paperwork, but he wanted to see the original detectives' case file—a task that would prove to be surprisingly difficult. There was no computer database or central storage room where it could be instantly located.

Instead, Bobby and I ended up in the bowels of the 9th Precinct's basement, in Manhattan, where we found ourselves in an abandoned jail cell surrounded by dozens of old brown cardboard boxes stacked haphazardly like a precarious Jenga tower. The sides of the boxes were marked with years scrawled in black marker: "1982–1984," "1987–1988." There was even one from 1931.

The elusive Palladium box was nowhere to be found, but Bobby didn't need the case folder to move his investigation forward. Among the first people he tracked down was Julie Brunner, who had been working as a coat check girl at the Palladium the night of the shootings. Markus Peterson had collapsed into her arms after being shot, and she'd seen the gunman. She didn't pick out Lemus or Hidalgo when she was shown a photo array with them in it, and she was never called to testify at their trial. Now, more than a decade later, I filmed the moment when Bobby and his partner, John Schwartz, showed her an array of several mug shots, including Lemus's, Hidalgo's, and Spanky's.

"I have a feeling about this guy," she said, pointing to a photo.

She selected Spanky. It obviously wasn't solid enough evidence to overturn a jury's verdict, but it was a sign to Bobby that he was still on the right track.

A couple of weeks later, in October 2002, I joined Bobby and John when they drove to visit Shawangunk Correctional Facility to interview former C&C gang member Joey Pillot. I was astonished that Pillot agreed to speak with them, especially because Bobby was the one who had arrested him. I was even more surprised when he consented to allow me to record their conversation. Pillot had nothing to gain, but it seemed that the universal respect Bobby commanded was shared even by those he had arrested. When we walked in, Pillot greeted him like an old friend.

In a prison conference room I sat at the end of a long table with my camera as Pillot, dressed in his prison greens, recounted what had happened that night at the Palladium. It was exactly the same story he'd told years earlier on the witness stand during that hearing in 1996: that Spanky and he were the Palladium gunmen.

"We're hanging out in the club," Pillot recounted, "a big commotion started with the bouncer. The bouncers grabbed Spanky and started beatin' up on him. They let him go and that's when the shooting started. We ran back to my car and drove back to the Bronx."

Pillot was under the impression that Lemus and Hidalgo had been released years earlier after he confessed, and he was visibly shaken when he learned they were still in prison.

"You dropped a bombshell on me," Pillot said, shaking his head. "I thought those kids was home." He said he'd never met Lemus or Hidalgo, adding, "The system sucks, man. They should let those kids go home. They know the truth; they just don't want to let those kids go home."

Bobby and John also tracked down David Lemus's old girlfriend Janice Catala. A police report from the week of David's arrest had claimed Janice had been interviewed and told detectives that she and Lemus were at the Palladium that Thanksgiving night.

"It puts Lemus at the scene of the crime," Bobby explained to me. "So, if he wasn't there, what's the explanation for the report?"

Janice had no idea Bobby and John were coming to her apartment or that I'd be in tow with a camera, but she agreed to allow me to film her conversation with the detectives.

Still in her pajamas, she sat on her unmade bed and described how in 1990 a detective had tried to convince her to sign a statement that she and Lemus had been at the Palladium that night, but she refused because it wasn't true.

"They kept telling me we were there," Janice remembered. "The cops kept on badgering me. I mean, they had me there for hours and I kept telling them no, we were not at the Palladium. We were home, we had Thanksgiving dinner, and we went to sleep."

That statement placing her and Lemus at the Palladium was written by a detective and never signed by Janice. But it was enough to discredit her as a witness, and she was never called to testify in Lemus's trial.

Bobby wanted to make clear what he was hearing.

"Wait, I just want to understand this because it's important. You never told them anything about going to the Palladium?" Bobby asked.

"No, I didn't say he was at the Palladium," Janice said with force. "The cops were the ones saying that."

As I filmed her saying this, Bobby and John seemed uncomfortable. They looked at my rolling camera and then exchanged nervous glances.

Bobby asked Janice, "When he was convicted of this murder, what was your feeling?"

"I couldn't believe it," she said. "I really couldn't believe it. I kept on saying, 'There's no way. He was with me.'"

I kept recording as we left the apartment and headed down the hallway toward the elevator. The discomfort of the two detectives was almost tangible. They knew what it meant.

"We had somebody telling us that one of our brother officers had basically perjured himself in a police report," Bobby said.

"This is like a scene from all those bad cop movies," John said nervously. "I've never been involved with anything like this before. The only place I'd ever seen it was in the movies."

"That was a very bad moment for me," Bobby would later say.

This was no longer just about Lemus and Hidalgo. This was about the truth and Bobby and John's solemn vow to protect the integrity of the system. Bobby had been convinced for many years that Lemus and Hidalgo were doing Spanky and Joey's time, and everything he was now learning proved it. Bobby knew he needed to do something.

5   THE BOSS

THE MAIN OFFICE FOR the Manhattan district attorney is located at One Hogan Place, near the southern tip of Manhattan not far from Wall Street. It is widely considered one of the most formidable law enforcement agencies in the country, in large part because of two men who served as Manhattan district attorney.

Frank Hogan, who first took office in 1942 and after whom the street is named, was New York City's top prosecutor for more than thirty years. Hogan's death in 1974 marked the end of one era and the dawn of another, when he was succeeded by Robert Morris Morgenthau. Over the course of the next thirty-five years, until his retirement in 2009 at the age of ninety, Morgenthau would be elected nine times, preside over some 3.5 million prosecutions, and be routinely referred to as a legend.

The son of Henry Morgenthau, a close friend of Franklin D. Roosevelt's who served for eleven years as secretary of the treasury, Robert Morgenthau was both loved and feared. For those working in the DA's office, Morgenthau was not just a boss, he was *the* boss, and getting hired by him was a privilege comparable to acceptance by an Ivy League school. Hundreds of smart, confident, smooth-talking prosecutors roamed lower Manhattan, helping to fight crime, getting convictions, "doing justice." But what if one of Morgenthau's millions of convictions was unjust? Bobby was learning that the DA's office didn't seem to want to hear about that. Yet after speaking with Joey Pillot and Janice Catala, he was more convinced than ever that justice hadn't been done.

And so, just as he had done a decade earlier, he made an appointment to discuss the Palladium case, yet again, with Manhattan prosecutor Stephen Saracco.

On the chilly evening of November 17, 2002, the night before his scheduled meeting with Saracco, I filmed Bobby, his partner, John, and a couple of other detectives on their team discussing strategy. With snow falling lightly outside, they sat in a conference room eating Chinese takeout and going over any possible scenario in which Bobby might encounter resistance.

Joey Pillot, who had repeatedly confessed, was already locked up. But Spanky was scheduled to be released in a few weeks from federal prison, where he was doing time for other C&C crimes.

"We wanted to lock him up for the Palladium shooting before his foot hit the pavement," said Bobby.

But because the Palladium murder happened in Manhattan, Bobby would need the permission of the Manhattan DA before he would be allowed to make an arrest. "Men of conscience have to do something," Bobby said. "Tomorrow we'll see if the truth lives."

The next morning, Bobby, John Schwartz, and their lieutenant from Bronx Homicide, Sean O'Toole, drove down to the Manhattan DA's office, picking me up at my apartment on the way, convinced that they were on the verge of freeing Lemus and Hidalgo. I jumped into the backseat next to Bobby with my camera and asked him how he was feeling.

"I'm ready," Bobby said. "I woke up this morning thinking it'd be a lot easier than I thought. The facts speak for themselves."

Carrying his brown cardboard box of evidence, and accompanied by John and their lieutenant, Bobby took the elevator to the sixth floor and headed to Saracco's office while I waited outside. Forty-five minutes later, I watched the three men walk out of the revolving door, looking like they'd been in there a week.

"That was a stone wall that we walked into!" Bobby blurted out. He felt Saracco was uninterested and dismissive of the evidence they presented, and John agreed.

"We were treated with such hostility from the time that we walked in," John said. "I have never been treated like that in nineteen and a half years in the police department."

Their boss, Sean O'Toole, felt it too. Standing outside on the street, he said to Bobby, "I don't know about you, but after sitting through that meeting, it would make me more determined about what I believe."

After the meeting, the four of us went to an Outback Steakhouse for lunch. Bobby, looking forlorn with a stack of fried onion rings in front of him, needed to talk it out. And we did, for a couple of hours. It sounded to me like Saracco seemed to take their request as a personal attack. But I also thought there may have been something else at play. By now I'd been embedded with Bobby and John for seven months and had spent hundreds of hours with them. The Bronx cops often talked as if they were in a different hemisphere from Manhattan, almost like there were two different police departments.

I wondered if the reaction they got was because of some unspoken turf battle. When Bobby told Saracco he wanted to arrest Spanky before he was released from federal custody the next month, Saracco told him to come back in a week with a formal report. So a week later I once again hitched a ride to the DA's office with the detectives as they delivered their report. This time when they arrived at Saracco's office, someone else was there: Dan Bibb, a veteran prosecutor.

I didn't have to wait long to hear how this meeting went. Bobby and John emerged less than fifteen minutes later.

"Saracco took the report from us, threw it onto his desk, thanked us, and that was pretty much it," John said.

Three weeks passed, and on December 17, 2002, Spanky was let out of prison in West Virginia and given a bus ticket back to New York. The next day I filmed an update with Bobby in Fort Apache as he sat at his desk describing his lack of communication with Saracco.

"We never heard a word back," Bobby said. "Nothing. Zero. We called him a couple of times. Never returned our calls. Not even the decency to say, 'Hey, Bobby, listen, you know, this isn't gonna happen before he gets out, unfortunately.' I'm at a loss for words. I'm at a loss about what to do next."

Bobby said he felt bad for Markus Peterson's family because he believed his killer, Spanky, was now back walking the streets. He felt sorry for Lemus's and Hidalgo's families, too.

I also found myself thinking more about David Lemus and Olmedo Hidalgo, which was why I had gone to Green Haven weeks earlier, on Thanksgiving morning, 2002, the twelfth anniversary of the murder for which they were convicted.

That day marked a before and after in my life. It was the day I first heard the name Jon-Adrian "JJ" Velazquez.

I'd gotten to know David Lemus's mother, Nilsa, and seen how she, like so many other mothers, dressed up to see her imprisoned son, with perfect makeup, and brought bags of homemade treats. I found her determination to present a brave front as endearing as it was heartbreaking, and my plan that Thanksgiving morning was to film an interview with her outside the prison after her visit.

I was walking into the prison's lobby when I was approached by Maria Velazquez, who'd been waiting for me, clutching the hands of her young grandsons, her eyes filled with despair, insisting her son JJ had been wrongfully convicted of murdering a retired NYPD officer. At that point JJ had been in prison for four years.

Maria explained that JJ and David Lemus had become friends at Green Haven and bonded over their mutual claims of innocence, and that they studied together in the prison's law library. I'd later find out that not only did they live in the same housing unit, but also their cells were next to each other. They shared the same concrete wall. And both of them had been prosecuted by the Manhattan DA's office during Morgenthau's tenure.

My initial reaction was pure skepticism and disbelief. I thought the Palladium was a one-in-a-million story. Even so, I said to Maria that she could send me any information she'd like, and I handed her my business card. A week later, a box of JJ's legal paperwork arrived at my NBC office, followed by a letter. It bore the distinctive markings of prison mail, tagged with his New York State Corrections Department–issued number, 00A2303.

DECEMBER 5, 2002

Dear Mr. Slepian,

Greetings.

I spend a lot of time trying to familiarize myself with the law. Monday through Thursday, anyone who knows me knows that I can be found in the law library. I know I don't belong here, but I am a firm believer that everything that happens to us in life is for a purpose. In no way am I condoning the injustice that has occurred in my life, but this incarceration has given me the opportunity to observe the world from another perspective. My mother has informed me that she has provided you with a copy of my trial transcripts. But it seems that your copy is incomplete. There were 2,044 pages in total. If I am correct, she has only provided you with 1,689 pages. In any event, if you don't have all the pages, we will make the necessary arrangements to get them to you. . . .

I'd received a good amount of prison mail over the years, but this letter stood out. If this guy was guilty, why would he be worried that I was missing 355 pages? My next thought was that I hardly had the time to read a 2,044-page trial transcript. But I did call and leave a message for Claudia Trupp, JJ's court-assigned appellate lawyer. A week later, another letter from JJ arrived.

DECEMBER 12, 2002

Dear Mr. Slepian:

Greetings.

The purpose of this letter is to inform you that Claudia Trupp from the Center for Appellate Litigation came up here to see me yesterday (12/11/02). She was honest in stating that if it had not been for your call, she would not have been up here to see me. Mrs. Trupp actually came up here to advise me of my rights, and to discourage my communication with you.

In any event, I made my position clear to her, and she respectfully accepted it. She seems to be a nice woman. She explained to me that as a member of the media you have no fiduciary obligations to me, and that if you were to come across damaging information and reveal it, that the District Attorney would be able to use it against me. I explained to her that I am 100% innocent of the crime I have been convicted of, and that I have no fear of any information you may find as you conduct your investigation. It would be senseless for me to ask anyone to thoroughly investigate this case knowing I took part in any of the events leading to my conviction. I came to you because I need help proving my innocence, and already your support got the ball rolling. Thank you. Although you have not made any commitments to me, you certainly have been helpful.

As I read JJ's letters, I thought, *Who is this guy?* His words flowed with perfect penmanship and methodical reasoning. He seemed philosophical and thoughtful. I didn't reply to any of the letters, but I was impressed by the man writing them and, honestly, slightly skeptical he'd composed them himself. Most of all, I still had trouble believing that I'd just happened to trip over another innocent guy in the same prison as Lemus and Hidalgo. It seemed too far-fetched to be true.

I was still consumed with the Palladium case, but I felt compelled to meet JJ. The day after that letter arrived, I went back to Green Haven to visit him. It was Friday, December 13, 2002. After being processed through security, JJ walked in. He stood about five foot nine, a few inches shorter than me. He was bald, with a finely shaven goatee, and he was wearing highly starched, state-issued prison greens. As we began to talk, it quickly became obvious that he had indeed written those thoughtful letters.

Of course, the fact that he was intelligent and wrote well didn't mean that he was innocent, but something about JJ's demeanor felt like it didn't align with the crime for which he had been found guilty: the murder of a retired police officer.

I told him I'd start reading through the thousands of pages that constituted his case when I could, but made sure to let him know that wasn't going to happen anytime soon. I made it clear that even if I discovered evidence of his innocence, the odds were slim that a story about him would turn into an hour on *Dateline*. And I told him that if I ever found out that he had lied to me about anything, even the color of his underwear, he'd never see me again. He didn't appear concerned. He said he had nothing to hide, and to my surprise, he challenged me to find him guilty.

Though I was intrigued by JJ and wanted to learn more about the details of his conviction, I had a dozen other personal and professional obligations that had to come first, and I knew that assessing the validity of his claim would involve thousands of hours of meticulous research. And even if I found compelling evidence, what I had told him about doing a segment on *Dateline* was true—even with everything I'd already documented in the Palladium case, I still hadn't gotten a green light to get that on TV.

Most of all, JJ's case seemed far murkier than that of Lemus and Hidalgo. In their case, I had, for starters, two well-respected, active-duty NYPD officers—Bobby Addolorato and John Schwartz—who had publicly declared that Lemus and Hidalgo were innocent. In JJ's case, on the other hand, there were no authority figures speaking out for him. Even his own attorney had advised him not to speak with me. And from the little I knew about his conviction, it appeared airtight. Police and prosecutors said five eyewitnesses had picked JJ out as the killer, and they also said that his alleged codefendant pleaded guilty and said he had committed the crime with JJ. I had no idea how he, or I, would ever be able to dispute that evidence. Still, I couldn't get JJ's voice out of my head, especially because the letters kept coming, and coming, and coming.

FEBRUARY 13, 2003

Dear Dan,

To be honest I am unsure of how to explain my troubles. The holidays hit me pretty hard this year. It was almost as if I had lost my entire spirit. I filled out cards at the very last minute, one of them being yours (enclosed), and just never got around to sending any of them out, except to my mother and children because they came up here to receive theirs. I even forgot to send my youngest son Jacob a card for his birthday, which is so unlike me. When I realized what I did, or rather failed to do, it hurt me deeply in my heart. I felt like such a terrible father. I still have not forgiven myself. I couldn't even put my usual mask on for my mother. She knew something was wrong. I just wanted to break down and cry, but I had to hold my composure because I am the strength of this family.

One month before JJ wrote me that letter, Jocelyn and I found out that she was pregnant and that I would soon become a father myself. JJ's letters touched me in a way I couldn't ignore, particularly when he wrote about the pain and heartbreak of missing his two sons.

Dear Dan,

 I am dealing with a whole lot of fear. Fear that I may never again retain my freedom. Fear that I may lose my children to the streets or the system before I can be there for them to save them . . .

 I filed everything JJ sent in a brown banker's box that sat on the floor in the corner of my office, along with the thousands of pages of court documents and transcripts his mom, Maria, had sent. I still had no clue about the details of JJ's case or if he was innocent, but it was hard not to be impressed both by his obvious character and by his unwavering persistence. One day I hoped to be able to start digging into the facts, but I knew that day wasn't even on the horizon.

 My daughter, Casey, would be born in September 2003, ushering in a new era of sleepless nights while I learned how to be a father. And I was still knee-deep in the Palladium story, which was about to blow up in Detective Bobby Addolorato's face.

 JJ's case would have to wait.

6   NO RETREAT, NO SURRENDER

BOBBY ADDOLORATO WAS A tough cop, but he had never been through anything like this. Feeling ignored by the Manhattan DA's office, and forced to stand by as Spanky Morales was released from prison, Bobby seemed defeated and increasingly depressed.

Being a cop was all Bobby had ever wanted to do, and he'd reached the highest rank an NYPD detective could achieve. He'd always worked well with others, yet the degree of disdain and contempt shown by the Manhattan prosecutors seemed to haunt him, especially because all he cared about was doing the right thing.

"I treat everybody with respect," Bobby said. "I expect at least from the DA's office to be treated with respect."

Still, he had not given up. As 2002 came to a close, he was on duty on Christmas Eve, and with the wind whipping up outside, my colleague Michelle Feuer filmed Bobby walking from the precinct to a nearby church to say a prayer for Lemus and Hidalgo.

"I swore an oath when I signed up with the police department to protect the rights of everybody, to uphold the Constitution," he later told me. "And I'll be damned if I'm going to sit by idly on my hands because it's convenient for me and because no one's going to give me a hard time if I just shut my mouth and let two guys rot in jail, and don't rock the boat. Well, the boat be damned."

Nearly a year had passed since I'd first learned about the Palladium murder, and with the saga having no end in sight, I was getting the sense my intense focus on the case was starting to annoy my bosses at NBC. I even started to call the story the "P-word" so they didn't have to hear me say the name of the nightclub so often.

My visits to the Bronx also became less frequent because I was back to traveling nearly every week, working on other stories. But whenever I was in New York I still filmed Bobby when I could, including on nights and weekends, even though there wasn't much to shoot because in early 2003 Bobby had been told he was being sidelined.

The Palladium case was reassigned to Manhattan detectives, and Bobby and John were ordered to spend a month in the Manhattan South precinct to help get their replacements up to speed. Despite his expertise and experience, when he got down there Bobby said he felt that he and John stood out like new kids at school—and his new classmates were not welcoming. He told me one Manhattan detective had a simple message for him: "Don't get comfortable. You won't be here long."

About a week after Bobby and John's arrival, the newly assigned Palladium team and their chief left for lunch, pointedly not inviting their Bronx colleagues. Alone in the precinct, Bobby opened up a box on one of the detectives' desks, and what he found made him dizzy. There, in Manhattan South, was the original Palladium case file. It wasn't lost somewhere in deep storage, as he'd assumed; they'd actually always had it in the Manhattan DA's office and never shared it with him.

But now here he was, holding original documents proving that detectives and prosecutors had known from the very beginning that Thomas "Spanky" Morales had been a suspect in Markus Peterson's killing. Most damning were notes that detectives had taken in the days after the murder describing how several bouncers had picked out Spanky's picture.

Normally the next step would have been to place Spanky in a live lineup, but that never happened.

Why not? One answer is a mistake made by Victoria Garcia, the lead detective on the case. When I spoke with her, she didn't seem nefarious, but she did sound confused. And how she handled the Spanky tip arguably set some of the chaos in motion.

"There were two Spankys, that's what the problem was," she said.

Garcia said she had been well aware that a "Spanky" had been named as a suspect, and she immediately ran that nickname through the NYPD's database. Among the people on the list that came back was a guy named Frankie Figueroa. (Figueroa would later be referred to as "Fat Spanky" in court filings.)

Garcia put "Fat Spanky" Figueroa's mug shot in a photo array and showed it to the eyewitnesses. Several picked him out as the heavyset guy in front of the Palladium who tried to mediate the dispute that ended in a murder. But there was a problem: Frankie Figueroa had been in jail on the night of the murder, so the eyewitnesses were wrong. Figueroa couldn't have been at the Palladium and couldn't have been involved in the shooting. He just happened to also go by the nickname "Spanky."

But there really had been a heavyset guy who was trying to mediate that night at the Palladium, except his name was not Spanky. It was Richie Feliciano, the informant in federal prison who had read the *New York Times* story in 2000 and called John O'Malley from the U.S. attorney's office to say he was at the Palladium and had mediated the fight with the bouncers, and to insist that the other Spanky—Spanky Morales—and Joey Pillot were the real gunmen.

The eyewitnesses had misidentified Figueroa as being at the scene, and when I saw his picture next to Richie Feliciano's, I understood why: they looked like brothers.

Detective Garcia never followed up on the right Spanky because the eyewitnesses had mistakenly identified a different one who could not have been the shooter, and that decision had huge repercussions.

Bobby found even more damning information in the file, like documentation that a Harlem snitch reported that Spanky Morales had bragged about the shooting shortly after it happened. And, unbelievably, there were handwritten notes from Detective Garcia, saying she had spoken with Spanky Morales's sister-in-law, Danila Troche, a US border agent, who told her that Spanky had tried to rape her. In reporting the attempted rape, Troche said her husband had told her that Spanky, his brother, had been the Palladium shooter, but Garcia never contacted Troche or her husband again. The notes were dated February 1991, one month after David Lemus was arrested, but apparently they had been kept from Lemus and Hidalgo's lawyers.

Bobby's mind flashed back to all the trips he'd made to the Manhattan DA's office and the evidence he'd amassed for more than a decade: bringing them his informant Benny Rodriguez in 1992, then Joey Pillot's confession in 1994, Richie Feliciano in 2000, the 911 tip call, and all the other leads over the years.

Now these documents proved to Bobby that the DA's office had even more information all along, and certainly should have known that it was Spanky and Joey Pillot who belonged in prison, not David Lemus and Olmedo Hidalgo.

I was in Las Vegas shooting an interview for a different story when I got Bobby's call.

"These lying sons of bitches knew they had the wrong guys the whole time!" he told me. "The DA's office knew that Spanky was an implicated shooter in this case over a decade ago."

I'd spoken with Bobby nearly every day for a year at this point, but on this day he sounded different, almost sick.

"They knew about it before the trial of Lemus and Hidalgo. The DA was full of crap when they cross-examined Joey Pillot in '96 and argued that he was making the story up. They knew then that the person he was accusing of doing this murder had been identified not long after the murder, so they were lying back then."

Bobby couldn't understand how this had happened. This was not his NYPD. The first thing he did after finding the file was contact the NYPD legal division for guidance, telling them he'd discovered crucial information that was never turned over to the defense. With that single call, the career he adored began to unravel.

When one of the bosses at Manhattan South found out Bobby had called the legal division, Bobby said he and John Schwartz were reprimanded for going outside Manhattan South and forbidden from making any more phone calls.

"I was screamed at like a child," said Bobby.

"We were ordered to remain silent," John remembered. "I said, 'You know what? If we're not gonna do anything down here, we'll go back to the Bronx.' And that's what we did. We went back to the Bronx."

The NYPD, the force Bobby had served faithfully for two decades, now treated him like a pariah. Not only was he breaking the blue wall of silence, but he was also suggesting that prosecutors at the country's most prestigious DA's office had deliberately withheld evidence from the defense, a serious accusation.

During the discovery process, which occurs before a trial, prosecutors were legally permitted back then to withhold any information from defense lawyers that they didn't deem relevant, but they were required to disclose to the defense any evidence that might be exculpatory. If prosecutors didn't turn over potentially important information, it was a serious infraction of a DA's constitutional obligation, a violation of the so-called Brady Rule—named for the Supreme Court's 1963 decision in *Brady vs. Maryland*—which was a cornerstone of fair trials. It also would be an ethical violation under the guidelines of the American Bar Association.

The most radical behavior Bobby had ever displayed was getting an ear pierced years earlier (though he never wore an earring) and listening to Bruce Springsteen too loud. Now he was painted as a troublemaker who needed to be watched.

Cops can lose their jobs for doing drugs, and the department has the right to give officers random drug tests. Not since 1985—almost twenty years earlier—had the NYPD summoned Bobby for a surprise drug test, but suddenly Bobby had four tests in three months, and he began to worry that he would be framed. He was also ordered to turn over a list of all his prescription drugs for the prior two years, and the detectives' union said unless he complied, the NYPD could take away his gun and badge and restrict him to desk duty. A friend, an inspector from the Bronx, warned Bobby to watch his back because the department was after him.

The walls were closing in, and Bobby became increasingly paranoid. He believed his phone was bugged and cut short conversations. He told me he kept looking over his shoulder or in his rearview mirror watching for a police tail.

With Bobby sidelined, David Lemus and Olmedo Hidalgo were left with a single legal lifeline who truly understood the intricate details of their convoluted ordeal: former assistant US attorney Steve Cohen, who was sitting next to Bobby in 1994 when Joey Pillot confessed to the Palladium murder. Now Cohen was in private practice and had agreed to represent the men pro bono.

One day I met Bobby at Steve Cohen's office next to Bryant Park in Midtown. When we walked into the conference room, Bobby made a beeline for the windows and closed the curtains.

"I'm being followed," he said.

"But we're on the forty-second floor," said Steve.

"They have helicopters," Bobby replied.

Despite the long, complicated history of the case, Steve was optimistic. In light of the new evidence Bobby had found, Steve believed he would finally be able to rectify what had become an obvious and glaring miscarriage of justice, and he hoped to work with the DA's office to do so, because if that strategy didn't pan out, he and a team of lawyers would have to spend hundreds of hours preparing and filing yet another motion to get Lemus and Hidalgo another hearing before a judge. Not only would that be an uphill battle and far from guaranteed to work, but it would also likely consume another year or longer.

So Steve Cohen met with the Palladium prosecutor, Stephen Saracco, and afterward told me how he thought it went.

"Saracco said to me, 'We'll look at it. I hear what you're saying. Give us six weeks and we'll get back to you. And then we'll all get together, sit down, hash it out.' And I say, 'Great.' I can't ask for more than that. And I leave that meeting feeling pretty good about where things stand."

The same wasn't true for Bobby. He felt horrible. One spring afternoon in 2003, I went up to the Bronx while he was on duty to check in with him. Walking through that wooden door of Bronx Homicide felt so different than it had the first day I showed up more than a year earlier. As I turned on my camera, I saw Bobby sitting at his desk looking confused, as if trying to comprehend how his career and character had been destroyed simply by trying to do the right thing. He told me he couldn't sleep and had begun snapping at his wife and kids.

"The DA's office stripped me of my dignity," Bobby said angrily. "They took my reputation, my credibility . . . Twenty years of working my ass off, I'm told I can't investigate a case, my opinion doesn't matter. They tell me I'm not allowed to say anything to anybody."

Later that day I filmed Detective Mike Donnelly, who was on Bobby's team, talking about Bobby's Palladium obsession: "I told him a long time [ago], put those boxes away and forget about them, because it's eaten him up!" Donnelly said. "It's taken the wind out of his sails. He's not the same guy." I found Donnelly's comments odd, given that two potentially innocent men were in prison.

And if I had known then what I'd learn ten years later about Donnelly's role in another case, I would have asked him way more questions.[1]

A few months later, Bobby lost his rock: his partner, John Schwartz. Disgusted by how they were treated over the Palladium case, John retired as soon as he hit twenty years on the job.

The Palladium had now become more than a story for me; it had become a window into a dark side of the justice system. And in the midst of it all was a broken cop. On the day he was ordered to stop investigating the Palladium case, Bobby wrote me about how it made him feel.

> What are they afraid of? Is it the possibility that they could be wrong? That they have done something that they are afraid of being caught having done? I'm not eloquent enough to express it in a way that makes sense but lately nothing makes sense to me. I feel very alone. I worry for two innocent men whose lives have been destroyed. Do I stay quiet and become one of the weak, morally corrupt people who put themselves first? Or fight for truth the way my parents raised me to? People who know me know the answer to this: No Retreat, No Surrender.

In late spring 2003, more than six weeks after Steve Cohen first met with Manhattan ADA Stephen Saracco, they got together again. Saracco told Cohen that the office had launched another reinvestigation into the Palladium convictions. What Saracco didn't say was that he would be retiring just weeks later, timing that Saracco later insisted was completely unrelated to the Palladium reinvestigation. Dan Bibb, Saracco's best friend in the office, would take over the Palladium case, and he'd be assisted by another veteran prosecutor, Joel Seidemann.

To Cohen's great frustration, Bibb said he was going to start his reinvestigation from the very beginning. Several more weeks passed. Cohen, believing the facts were clear, thought the investigation would soon be wrapping up. He began leaving messages for Bibb, trying to get an update.

A few days later, Bibb left Cohen a voicemail message: "All I can tell you is it's not my job to keep you up to speed on exactly what we're doing. What I can tell you is that the investigation is proceeding. There are interviews happening every day. I can also tell you that the investigation is not going to take weeks. It's going to take months. If that's unfortunate for you, I apologize. But I have other obligations in the office besides this case."

After hearing Bibb's message, Steve called me and told me to come to his office with my camera. He was fuming. "It's pathetic because we're dealing with two human lives! People who I believe didn't do anything and are now sitting in jail for more than a decade. And are being told basically through me, 'We'll get to it when we get to it'!"

As it turned out, Dan Bibb's reinvestigation of the Palladium murder didn't take months. In all, it would take more than a year and a half, during which time Bibb traveled to more than a dozen states and interviewed about fifty people, mostly C&C gang members.

In the meantime, Bobby went downtown to One Police Plaza to turn in his shield and his gun. His ID now read RETIRED. Standing in front of police headquarters on his last day as an NYPD officer, with Lemus and Hidalgo still in prison, a dejected Bobby said to me, "It's like leaving the house with the coffeemaker on."

As the months passed, I worked on other stories for *Dateline* that had actual airdates, but I kept filming for a future Palladium show whenever I could, having no idea if, how, or when this was ever going to end. During this time, I was also speaking with the Palladium's new prosecutor, Dan Bibb, on the phone every few weeks, and we occasionally went to lunch.

He said the Palladium reinvestigation was the toughest case of his career, particularly because as he spoke with more witnesses, it became increasingly difficult for even him to ignore the mountain of evidence that demonstrated that two innocent men were wasting away in prison. Finally, sometime in spring 2004, Bibb told me that he had come to his own conclusion: the shooters were Spanky and Pillot, not Lemus and Hidalgo.

Holy shit! I thought. *This is the* prosecutor *saying this. This means they're out, right?*

Not so fast.

Bibb told me that he shared his views in briefings he gave his bosses, but they said there was insufficient basis for them to support overturning the convictions. They did agree to have a new hearing for a judge to make that decision, but Bibb was not happy. He didn't want to stand in court and defend convictions he didn't believe were just. But that's exactly what he did.

Incredibly, there was someone else who didn't dispute Bibb's take: his best friend, the original Palladium prosecutor, Stephen Saracco.

By now, I'd had lunch a few times with Saracco and had also spoken with him on the phone. During one call in September 2004, I asked him why he tried to keep Lemus and Hidalgo behind bars even after there was so much evidence that they were innocent.

He said of Lemus that there was a "stink around him . . . There were too many coincidences in there that just bothered me."

Then I pressed him about why Hidalgo was charged as Lemus's codefendant when no one could even connect the men. Saracco told me: "Hidalgo was always like the caboose at the end of all the arguments."

When I said no one seemed to have tried to connect Lemus and Hidalgo, Saracco pushed back: "Oh, there was a big effort. We never could."

I'm not sure if he realized how ridiculous it sounded that he would prosecute two men for murder whom he couldn't connect to each other, but then he said something else that nearly knocked the wind out of me. "I don't know if they're innocent or guilty now," he said, but added: "There were twelve New Yorkers who said they were guilty. We had a trial. The jury rendered their verdict. Things came up. We aired them out. The judge denied it. Whatever hype is just media bullshit."

I told him that I'd finally gotten a green light from my bosses to do an hour-long show about the case, and that it would likely air soon. He said he wasn't interested in being a part of it.

I also asked the question that I could never seem to get a good answer to: "If Dan Bibb, the prosecutor, believes they're innocent, why are they still in prison?"

His answer barely made sense to me but reinforced why everyone told me Saracco was so good on his feet in court: "You are too indoctrinated and knee-jerk with this. It's not a matter of a position of they're innocent or guilty. There are positions being taken. There are people being interviewed and there were reports being filed. You know this is America. Don't you understand this is America?"

No, I didn't understand that word salad. Is this how the system really works? A homicide detective and a prosecutor were pointing out that two obviously innocent men were languishing in prison, but they couldn't get anyone to pay attention, even though they knew who the real killers were. Even after all these years, I still have trouble wrapping my mind around that. Saracco kept telling me that he was inclined to believe they were innocent but that it didn't matter, because it wasn't up to him to let anyone out of prison; only a judge could do that.

At the end of our half-hour call, Saracco said he'd enjoyed talking to me. "You're a good guy," he said. "How's your baby doing?"

I told him Casey was doing well and thanked him for asking. When I first showed up at Bronx Homicide and learned about the Palladium, Casey hadn't yet been conceived. Now she was walking and babbling. How old would she be by the time Lemus and Hidalgo got out?

7   FINDING SPANKY

LIKE BOBBY, ATTORNEY STEVE Cohen was made to suffer for his work on the Palladium case. The more he pushed, the more Manhattan prosecutors questioned his ethics, accusing him of a conflict of interest by helping Lemus and Hidalgo using what they called his "insider knowledge" of the federal C&C gang case from when he'd served as an assistant United States attorney.

"Suddenly I find myself in a position that is very similar to Bobby's," said Steve. "Not just very isolated but a sensation that the DA's office is circling the wagons."

Steve didn't want to become a distraction, so he decided to enlist the help of two other lawyers—Gordon Mehler and Daniel Horwitz—to represent Lemus and Hidalgo while he helped them from behind the scenes. It took months for the new attorneys to get up to speed, but on July 16, 2004, they filed a motion to vacate Lemus and Hidalgo's convictions based on newly discovered evidence and Brady violations.

Three days later I produced a story for WNBC about the newly filed motion. A voice-over boomed into millions of New York–area homes:

> It happened fourteen years ago at the once-popular Palladium nightclub on East Fourteenth. A fight broke out and two bouncers were shot. . . . An open-and-shut case? Maybe not. For the first time, you will hear evidence that the jury never heard—including another man who has since confessed to the crime and an eyewitness who backs up his story.

One of the people who was watching that segment was Carol Kramer, an editor at *New York* magazine who had been the jury forewoman in Lemus and

Hidalgo's trial and voted to convict. She got in touch with me, saying she felt devastated by what she now saw as a miscarriage of justice.

"I said, 'Wrongful conviction? How could that be?' It turned me upside down. I thought I'd been hit in the stomach. They didn't even know each other, and they didn't speak the same languages. The whole case was posited on the fact that these two men went to a club together, that they conspired to come back shooting. If they couldn't speak the same language, how could any of it be true? And I was really shocked. No, we didn't hear all the facts. If we had known them, we never would have convicted."

For more than a decade she had never questioned her guilty vote. Now she did, and it made her rethink her whole experience as a juror.

"That day I felt like a good American. The jury system works. I participated in it. You know? How many other things do you do to be a good citizen? You vote and you pay your taxes. The jury system seems like the most basic way you can be a citizen. And I went on with my life for the next twelve years totally sure that we had done the right thing."

Lemus and Hidalgo's motion to vacate their convictions was assigned to New York Supreme Court judge Roger Hayes. Dan Bibb and Joel Seidemann from the Manhattan DA's office opposed the motion to vacate the convictions but consented to a hearing. Bibb offered a different theory than Saracco had at the original trial, now acknowledging that Spanky was involved but insisting that didn't mean Lemus and Hidalgo were innocent. It meant, he said, that there were *three* perpetrators.

I knew that even Bibb didn't believe the argument he was making, but I still had a responsibility to find out if the three men knew one another. After all, this was now the official position of the Manhattan DA. I'd have to track down Spanky. Finding him was a challenge, but I eventually located him in Brooklyn, where he was living with his girlfriend. I reached him through her and began talking to him as the investigation unfolded. A couple of times I sent a car to pick him up, but he wouldn't get in. Finally, after the DA filing identified him as that third shooter, Spanky's curiosity was piqued and he arrived at 30 Rockefeller Plaza: a black hat on backward, a leather jacket, saggy jeans, eyes darting around as he smoked a cigarette.

Despite his criminal history, there was something about Spanky I could respect. Yes, he was likely a killer, but he made it clear he wasn't pretending to be anything else. He lived a life of crime, but he admitted it.

"I'm just saying that I came on my own free will," he said as I filmed our conversation. "You know, I'm not hiding it from nobody. They know where I'm at. They saying that they got an abundance of evidence that I have something involved with this, um, with this thing, you know, and I'm at the same place where I've been at since I've been home. So, and I just want to rectify and make it clear in the record that *I don't know these guys.*"

Judge Roger Hayes began hearing arguments on January 18, 2005. For the DA's office, Dan Bibb advanced an absurd new theory of the crime—that Lemus and Hidalgo had acted in concert with C&C gang member Spanky Morales even though all three men said they didn't know one another.

Judge Hayes asked Bibb if he had any proof there was a connection between Lemus, Hidalgo, and the C&C gang.

"Only in a tenuous way," Bibb replied. "After extensive efforts, I have not come up with information that connects either defendant with each other or with members of the C&C gang."

Judge Hayes then asked for an explanation for Spanky's continued freedom.

"It's the subject of continuing discussion in my office," said Bibb, almost mumbling.

Two weeks after that court date, my hour-long report, "Murder at the Palladium," finally aired nationally on *Dateline*. Stone Phillips, the show's anchor at the time, presented the story—and it sparked an unexpected chain of events.

8

THE HEARING

FIFTEEN YEARS AFTER THE Palladium murder and eight weeks after my *Dateline* hour aired showing my interview with Spanky Morales, the Manhattan DA indicted him for murder, claiming that he had acted in concert with Lemus and Hidalgo. On April 18, 2005, Spanky was arraigned, the very same morning David Lemus and Olmedo Hidalgo's hearing officially began in another courtroom down the hall.

Richard Verchick, Spanky's lawyer, would later file a motion with the court asking for the charges to be thrown out. In his filing, Verchick didn't claim Spanky was innocent, only that the DA had taken too long to bring the case against him. He cited a case in which the New York Court of Appeals ruled that there must be good cause for a district attorney to wait before charging someone when there was overwhelming evidence from the outset that the person was guilty.

Verchick detailed all the information that came to the attention of the NYPD and Manhattan DA's office over the course of fifteen years, beginning with that 911 call days after the murder. Remember, this motion was written by *Spanky's* defense attorney:

> The people had a Crimestoppers call implicating 'Spanky' and Joey . . . in 1992, they had C&C informant Benny Rodriguez saying he saw the crime happen, many tips from known sources concerning admissions that Joey and Spanky were responsible for the Palladium shooting, and four photo identifications by the same witnesses deemed reliable enough to be used to convict Lemus and Hidalgo.

Yet, his brief also pointed out, "nothing more was ever done to investigate 'Spanky' Morales. His whereabouts were always known . . . yet the people—doggedly it seems—persisted in not arresting him, not placing him in any lineup and not following up on these leads in any way. . . . At some point, one is forced to the conclusion that the DA's office simply did not want to know."

In his motion, Verchick suggested the reason Spanky was never arrested was that prosecutors didn't want to risk undermining the case against Lemus and Hidalgo: "Not only do we now have a powerful motive for the egregious persistence of the Manhattan DA in not arresting Spanky, but we also now have what we all must confront—bad faith."

It was a bold move: essentially saying, *You should have known I was the killer a long time ago. You missed your chance.*

And it worked.

Judge Bonnie Wittner dismissed the case in a scathing opinion that said the prosecution had "steadfastly ignored the mounting evidence that either the wrong men had been convicted and that Thomas 'Spanky' Morales, not Lemus or Hidalgo, was the real shooter, or at the very least, that Morales was the man who had the initial fight with the bouncer and was involved with the shooting. The People's inexcusable and inordinate delay in prosecuting Spanky Morales," she said, "compels the court to grant this motion."

The case against Spanky was over, but meanwhile Lemus and Hidalgo were serving their fifteenth year in prison. And now that their hearing was under way, they were being held at Rikers Island, New York's notoriously violent jail complex, from which they were shuttled back and forth to the courthouse at 111 Centre Street.

Dan Bibb wasn't thrilled to be the front man for the DA's office; he didn't believe Lemus or Hidalgo was guilty. But deep down he was a company man. His company was the Manhattan district attorney's office, and the chairman and CEO was Robert Morgenthau. After twenty-plus years of loyal service to the company, Bibb was conflicted. He didn't want to say no to prosecuting the two men, even if he believed he should, so together with his cocounsel, ADA Joel Seidemann, he argued the official position of the Manhattan DA's office—that the original convictions were good ones.

In the courtroom, David's mother, Nilsa, sat with Carol Kramer, the jury forewoman who had initially voted to convict her son but was now fighting for his release. Because the defense filed the motion, they were the first to question witnesses, starting with former Palladium bouncer James Callahan.

Callahan had confronted the shooter when he tried to reenter the club. Police interviewed Callahan the night of the shooting—and then, astonishingly, nobody in the case contacted him for another fourteen years, until Dan Bibb called. Bibb had met with Callahan during his reinvestigation and showed him a photo array, with pictures of Lemus, Hidalgo, Joey Pillot, and Spanky. Callahan quickly passed over the photographs of Lemus and Hidalgo and identified Spanky as the man he thought he had punched that night. Two days after his interview with Bibb, Callahan testified that he'd seen the WNBC story I'd done. After watching it, he said, he was certain that Spanky was indeed the shooter.

The defense then called bouncer Fritz Vincent, who had punched the gunman. At Lemus and Hidalgo's trial, Vincent had testified about what had happened but didn't identify Lemus as the person he had fought with. But now Vincent testified that seeing my interview with Spanky on *Dateline* jarred his memory. He said Spanky's facial expressions, body movements, and way of speaking convinced him he was the shooter.

Other witnesses who testified for Lemus and Hidalgo included Joey Pillot, who maintained, as he had for more than a decade, that he and Spanky were the gunmen, and that neither Lemus nor Hidalgo had any involvement in the crime.

Prosecutors Bibb and Seidemann called two witnesses: a pair of cousins, one of whom knew Pillot and the other of whom knew Lemus—apparently the closest connection they could find between the men.

The hearings dragged on, a day here and there, over the course of six months. Then, in late July 2005, the DA's office abruptly announced it was dropping the case against Hidalgo. But he never got the chance to leave the courtroom a free man. As soon as he was vindicated, Hidalgo was put back in handcuffs and deported to the Dominican Republic on the grounds that he'd been previously convicted on a gun charge and was in the country illegally.

But Bibb and Seidemann pressed on, continuing to argue that Lemus's motion should be denied and that his conviction should stand.

On October 19, Judge Roger Hayes announced his decision about David Lemus. That morning, I filmed former detective Bobby Addolorato, Lemus's unlikely advocate, as he met Nilsa, David's mother, for the first time. They hugged and Nilsa wept. As they walked to the courthouse, arm in arm, Bobby whispered, "Let's hope this is the day all our lives start again."

Before announcing his decision, Judge Hayes praised the lawyers for their dignified conduct, then turned his attention to David Lemus. "Mr. Lemus," he said, "your motion to vacate your convictions of murder and attempted murder based on newly discovered evidence is granted."

David bowed his head and began sobbing. His mother did too. Bobby reached over and patted her back. Next to him, the forewoman of the original jury, Carol Kramer, who'd been aghast when she found out about the concealed evidence, smiled and welled up with tears.

As I watched David begin to walk toward the courtroom door to take his first steps of freedom in fifteen years into the arms of his mother, emotion flooded over me as well. It was a moment that transcended words—a combination of relief and disbelief, as well as anger, and an overwhelming sense of joy.

Outside the courtroom, Nilsa's cries could be heard down the hall as she clung to her son. Bobby hung back behind the cameras, looking on and smiling.

"Good luck," Bobby said, hugging Lemus. "Do something good with your life."

"I owe you my life," Lemus said.

And as we walked away together, the cop who had had a suspicion, pursued it against all odds, and quit his job because of it told me, "I can truly say this was the highlight of my career."

But in fact, it wasn't over yet. Lemus wasn't free and clear. After fifteen years, three investigations, two hearings, and one trial, the Manhattan district attorney's office was, inconceivably, going to retry Lemus for murder. Dan Bibb said he was disgusted by the whole ordeal and decided to retire. Joel Seidemann was now the prosecutor in charge of trying to send an innocent man back to prison.

As I'm writing these words, I still can hardly believe it.

Within hours of his release, David Lemus boarded a flight and headed to Florida—though he was born in New York, the city didn't feel like home anymore. He got a job at a car dealership and tried to rebuild his life, which is not easy when you're facing trial again for a murder you clearly didn't do. He had to wait two full years before prosecutor Joel Seidemann would try to convince a jury to find him guilty again.

This time, Judge Bonnie Wittner would oversee the proceedings, which began in November 2007. I was there every day during the nearly three-week retrial, where I would learn another surprising lesson: the jury would not be allowed to know that Lemus had been convicted before, that it had been overturned, or that he already had spent fifteen years in prison. The reason? It would be prejudicial to the *prosecution* because it had nothing to do with what happened on the night of the murder.

Perhaps the most important witness for Lemus was Spanky Morales, who testified that he and Joey Pillot were responsible for killing Markus Peterson. When the acquittal came on December 6, 2007, after two days of deliberations, Lemus broke down in tears. He didn't want to speak to the group of reporters waiting for him outside, so he asked me to tell them that he was "savoring this moment."

Dan Bibb followed the case from afar. After leaving the DA's office, Bibb at first kept his feelings to himself, but when he started looking for work as a defense attorney, he discovered the DA's office was badmouthing him around town as a lawyer who could not be trusted.

His way of earning a living threatened, Bibb went public. He spoke with me for an updated, two-hour version of the Palladium case for *Dateline*. A year later, in 2008, in a front-page *New York Times* article—"Doubting Case, a Prosecutor Helped the Defense"—he portrayed himself as a secret angel for the two innocent men and claimed he threw the case for Lemus and Hidalgo.

There was a lot of fallout. The Manhattan district attorney's office filed a complaint with the state bar against Bibb. The story made Bobby furious; and in the *Times* story, Bobby's former partner, John Schwartz, made it clear what he thought of Bibb—a prosecutor who "effectively took part in keeping two innocent men in prison an additional year at least, for not going with what he felt was the truth."[1]

Why did Bibb handle the case the way he did? Here is his own explanation, in a letter to the bar's disciplinary authorities:

I felt that I had a number of choices. The first was to resign. While I am sure it would have garnered a lot of press coverage, it would not have moved the matter along to a just conclusion. In fact, it most likely would have substantially delayed the matter, resulting in the continued incarceration of two innocent men.

The next was insubordination, refusing to do the hearing and risk being fired. Practically speaking, neither of these was an option because I have a wife, three children, a mortgage and college tuition to pay and could not afford to be out of work. The last was to do exactly what I did, what every prosecutor should do: I worked to ensure a just result consistent with my conscience, ethical principles, and the evidence.

The day I was ordered to do the hearing was the worst day of what was then a 22½ year career as a prosecutor. After I left work that day, I called a friend and got together for a few drinks with him. . . . I mulled over and discussed with my pal resigning in protest, refusing to walk into the courtroom and letting them fire me or throwing the hearing. . . . I decided then that's what I would do.

Steve Cohen, bruised by his experience fighting against the Manhattan DA's office to get Lemus freed, wasn't having Bibb's supposed heroism. "Anybody who knows anything about criminal law," he told me, "will agree that there is something broken if that is the impression of the assistant district attorneys, that you do what you're told."

Then, fighting back tears, Steve said, "Overall, though, you walk away from this, and you know that not a lot's going to change because the DA's office doesn't want to hear it. There is a kind of arrogance that comes with that power. And it only expresses itself rarely, and so people think it's not much of a problem. But the reality is that in those rare occasions, it involves a human being."

I'm not a lawyer like Steve Cohen, but I thought it took real courage for Dan Bibb to be honest about believing in Lemus and Hidalgo's innocence. Bibb stood in court defending the convictions while believing they were innocent, but I believe him when he says that he was in an impossible position.

Dateline's updated Palladium documentary, which ran two hours, aired on August 5, 2007. It was about Lemus and Hidalgo, yes, but also about Bobby, and how he was swiftly destroyed by the very system that he had always re-vered. To me, Bobby remains a moral compass, and a profoundly ethical man who always fights for what he believes in the face of adversity.

The Palladium case was my baptism into the world of wrongful convictions, and it left me in utter disbelief at how this Kafkaesque narrative had unfolded over five long years. I had never fathomed that individuals within the system could brazenly disregard factual evidence.

Little did I know I was just scratching the surface.

9   "I TOLD YOU I'D BE BACK"

IN THE FIVE YEARS since I'd first met JJ, I had received a stack of letters from him, and we'd occasionally spoken on the phone. It was finally time to see if there was any truth to what he was telling me. On August 7, 2007, two days after my two-hour Palladium documentary aired on NBC and five years after I began my education in wrongful convictions, I went to interview JJ for the first time on camera, not at Green Haven but at Sing Sing, the notorious maximum-security prison about forty miles north of Manhattan, where he had been transferred.

Built two hundred years ago, Sing Sing was the first prison to be called "the Big House." Walking through the housing units, you can see why. It's home to one of the largest cell blocks in the country. Tiny cages run the length of two football fields, stacked four tiers high. It feels more like a warehouse than housing fit for any living creature. When I first saw it, I thought, *This is a place I wouldn't even board my dogs.*

After being processed through security, I picked up my camera gear and was led to a small conference room, located behind several locked gates. About five minutes later, JJ came in, escorted by two corrections officers.

"I told you I'd be back," I said.

"It's great to see you," JJ said with a smile.

He told me that he and dozens of other incarcerated men watched my show about the Palladium on a TV outside in the prison yard. "It brought a tear to my eye," JJ said. "Seeing David walk free was beautiful. I am him, and he is me. It gave me hope."

By then, I'd finally read through the police reports and all 2,044 pages of JJ's trial transcript, so I had a good sense of the details of the crime, which all sides agreed were facts.

* * *

The murder for which JJ had been convicted and sentenced to twenty-five years to life had happened nine and a half years before, on January 27, 1998, at 125th Street and Frederick Douglass Boulevard, the heart of Harlem. At around noon, two men barged into an illegal betting parlor run by a former NYPD officer named Albert Ward and announced a stickup. One of the men had a roll of duct tape and the other brandished a gun.

There were nine patrons in the betting parlor, all regulars. The place was on the second floor, above a barbershop, and had two rooms. In the front room, the man with the duct tape began to bind and rob the patrons, while his accomplice with the gun ventured into the back room, where he found twenty-year-old Augustus Brown selling heroin to forty-five-year-old Lorenzo Woodford. The gunman ordered Brown and Woodford to join the rest of the terrified patrons sprawled on the floor in the front room, and it was at that moment that Al Ward drew his own gun and engaged in a brief struggle with the man holding the duct tape.

The duct-taping man yelled, "He's got a gun, he's got a gun!" That prompted his partner to fire a shot into Al Ward's head, instantly killing him.

The two robbers fled the chaotic scene. Two other people took off right behind them—Augustus Brown, the heroin dealer, and his customer, Lorenzo Woodford.

Al Ward's murder was Harlem's first of 1998, a time in New York when the NYPD was Mayor Rudolph Giuliani's army, laser-focused on fulfilling his command to bring crime numbers down, especially murders. Since he had taken office four years earlier, homicides had been reduced by nearly 50 percent.

Because Ward was a former "MOS" (member of service), a steady stream of officers from the 28th Precinct, where Ward had once worked, began arriving on the scene. Within hours, high-ranking NYPD brass also responded. This was personal—one of their own, a brother in blue from the 28th. Never mind that he was running an illegal game; once a cop, always a cop, especially if he'd once worked in the same precinct that was now investigating his murder.

Robert Jones, who was guarding the door for Ward that day, told the detectives how it all went down. He said that around noon a stranger sought entry, claiming he was from the St. Nicholas Houses across the street. Jones let the man inside, and he filled out a betting slip, writing "Tee" as his name, and left.

About an hour later, Tee returned, this time, Robert said, brandishing a gun and accompanied by a partner holding a roll of duct tape. The two men barged in yelling, "Where is the money?"

According to the police report, Robert described the shooter as a "male black, light skinned, with a light beard and mustache" and "braids." Robert also said the shooter's accomplice with the duct tape was a "brown skinned guy a little darker than my brother."

Phillip Jones, Robert's brother, who also worked at the numbers spot, described the shooter slightly differently. He said the gunman was a "male, black, light-skin, red hair."

A third witness, Dorothy Canady, an eighty-six-year-old regular at the parlor, said she looked the shooter "dead in the face" and described him as "male black, light skinned, and wearing a dark green knitted hat."

Still another witness, Joe Scott, also said the gunman was Black, "very light-skinned," wearing "a black knit hat with braided hair sticking out."

After interviewing the witnesses, the NYPD broadcast an all-points bulletin, describing the shooter as a light-skinned Black man with braids. A sketch was made and distributed on a WANTED poster that listed the shooter as "male, black," with "braided hair, light complexion, thin mustache/beard."

Police killings are treated differently from other murders. If a cop-killer is on the loose, no one rests until an arrest is made, so a mobile command unit was immediately deployed to Harlem, staffed by four lieutenants, eight sergeants, and thirty-seven police officers. Their orders were to conduct "enforcement activity" in the area—in other words, shake up the neighborhood to legally detain and question as many people from the street as possible to elicit any information about the shooting.

Young men who matched the description of the suspect—a light-skinned Black man with braids—were stopped and questioned. Within twenty-four hours, more than 150 people were detained for minor offenses, all in an effort to interrogate as many people as possible who might know something.

I read in the police reports that the day after the murder, a man who was arrested for drug possession was shown the sketch of the shooter and said he knew him as "Mustafa." He said he'd heard from a friend that Mustafa had murdered someone at a numbers spot and had spent time at the St. Nicholas projects and a numbers hole on the East Side.

Then, another man charged with a drug offense told detectives that he was at a smoke shop when he heard people talking about how someone named Mustafa had shot a guy at a nearby numbers spot, and that one of them said, "That motherfucker is crazy." He said Mustafa sold blue bags of crack near the location of the shooting and that he thought Mustafa lived in the St. Nicholas projects.

Forty-eight hours after Al Ward's murder, the commander of the 28th Precinct wrote a memo to police brass declaring that Mustafa was their "primary target."

Meanwhile, detectives brought eyewitnesses to the precinct to look at mug shots of people who had been arrested in the area who matched the description of the suspects. Trying to identify a suspect this way is known as "trawling," and has been shown to result in an increased risk of misidentification. Think of it as looking for a needle in a haystack, without knowing if the needle is even in there.

First, witness Robert Jones was shown photos of light-skinned Black men based on his description of the shooter. But he changed that description as he looked at mug shots, saying, he "felt that the perp was half black and half Hispanic." Ultimately, he said mug shots of "white Hispanics" looked most like the shooter. He said he didn't see the gunman in any of the pictures he was shown.

Then police showed Jones mug shots of dark-skinned Black men in an effort to identify the shooter's accomplice. Eventually Jones pointed to a photograph of a man named Derry Daniels, and said he was the dark-skinned assailant binding people with the duct tape.

"That's the guy," Jones said to the lead detective, Joseph LiTrenta.

Derry Daniels was thirty-three years old, with at least eleven prior arrests, including another numbers-spot robbery, and he was immediately picked up. He denied any involvement in the shooting, saying he had been home at the time of the robbery and then had gone to meet a friend to smoke crack. Detective LiTrenta wasn't convinced and put Daniels in a lineup. After being identified by Robert and Phillip Jones as the shooter's accomplice, Daniels was placed under arrest.

Meanwhile, as police conducted a citywide hunt for their shooter, nicknamed Mustafa, they were also searching for Augustus Brown and Lorenzo Woodford, the two eyewitnesses who had fled after the shooting. They found Woodford first. Homeless and a drug addict with a criminal history dating back to 1964, Woodford admitted that he had been at the betting parlor to buy heroin from Augustus Brown, and that he injected "two to three" bags of heroin "every day." In fact, after he fled the scene, he said the first thing he did was get high and watch from across the street as police arrived. He said he fled after the shooting because he didn't want to be involved.

Like all of the other eyewitnesses, Woodford described the gunman as a light-skinned Black man who "might have had braids." Detectives then put Woodford in the back of a police car and drove him around Harlem to look for his dealer, twenty-year-old Augustus Brown. They found him on the street, selling drugs.

Brown had a criminal record that included convictions for drugs and criminal impersonation, and an arrest for robbery. Detectives escorted him to the 28th Precinct, where they found ten bags of heroin in his underwear and questioned him for hours.

In his interview, Brown confirmed he had been selling heroin to Lorenzo Woodford at Al Ward's place, and he provided the same version of what happened as the other witnesses, as well as a similar description of the shooter as a light-skinned Black man. Brown never suggested in this interview that he recognized the shooter or had ever seen him before.

Detectives then sat Brown in front of a computer screen to view mug shots of suspects. According to police reports, after viewing "a total of 230 pages of photos with eight photos per page," more than eighteen hundred pictures, Augustus Brown selected photo 9008803 as the gunman, but "stated that the color of his eyes look different on the computer screen."

The man Brown picked out as the shooter was Jon-Adrian Velazquez. Despite the fact that every eyewitness, including Brown, described the shooter as a "light-skinned black man," Brown was somehow shown a photo of JJ, who was listed as "white Hispanic" in the police database.

It was only after selecting JJ's picture that Brown added a key detail: "The witness then stated that he remembers that the perpetrator hung out on West Ninety-Fifth and West Ninety-Sixth and Amsterdam Ave and sold drugs there."

Police now had a new primary target. Just like that, the search for Mustafa ended, and the hunt for JJ—a Latino man who'd never had braids—began.

10   74 MINUTES

ON THAT HOT SUMMER day in 2007 when I first interviewed JJ in Sing Sing, I was very direct. "I'm a journalist, not your friend," I told him. "If I find anything that proves your guilt, it's coming out. I'm reporting it. The truth is all I care about. That's what I'm the advocate for. Not for you."

It was crucial for JJ to understand that my interest was always in the truth, regardless of its implications. I also made it clear to him that I would be asking him questions about matters I already knew about, just to see if he was lying to me. Another strategy I didn't share: I'd revisit questions over time to see whether his account changed or remained consistent.

JJ began to tell me his side of the story, how he got involved with all of this. He said he had grown up in a loving environment as a young child in Queens, cherished by both of his parents, who separated when he was eleven. His mother, Maria, was a union labor organizer who later moved to Haverstraw, in Rockland County, New York. His father, Adrian, was an Amtrak police officer. Adrian moved in with another woman in Manhattan and had a son with her, JJ's half brother.

As a child, JJ excelled academically and was an altar boy at his church. But when he became a teenager, things began to take a turn for the worse. At sixteen, he said, he started skipping school and hanging out with the wrong crowd, and his mother asked him to move in with his father in Manhattan. But things only got worse there, and he ended up dropping out of high school and dealing drugs.

When he was seventeen, he started dating Vanessa Cepero, a girl he knew from his neighborhood, and before long they had two children. Their first son, Jon Jr., arrived in 1994, when JJ and Vanessa were both nineteen. Three years later, Jacob was born.

By the end of January 1998, five weeks after Jacob's birth, JJ was living in the Bronx with Vanessa and their two boys. He told me that becoming a father transformed his perspective on life and fueled his determination to build a better future for his family. He wanted to become a role model for his sons. He enrolled in a technical college to study computer programming, but at night he was still selling drugs.

"I needed to put food in my children's mouths," JJ said.

He told me that the moment he learned he was wanted for the murder of Al Ward will forever remain etched in his mind. He was at home in the Bronx on January 30, 1998, a Friday, making breakfast and looking after his two boys, when his mother called him in a state of panic. She said the police were looking for him.

"I had no idea what they wanted," JJ said. "The only thing I could think of was the Albany case." Six months earlier, he had been arrested on drug charges in Albany, New York, and he was out on bail. But JJ had never been convicted of a crime, so why was his mug shot in the New York City system in the first place? It was one of the first questions I asked him.

He explained that a year earlier, he had been shopping at the Gap in Manhattan and came out carrying several bags. An officer followed him out of the store, convinced he was shoplifting. JJ had receipts for everything, but the cop used that stop as a pretense to search the car, and in the glove compartment he found small amounts of marijuana and cocaine. JJ was arrested, but the case was ultimately dismissed after a judge ruled it had been an illegal search and seizure. The case was sealed, and JJ's mug shot should have been removed from the NYPD's database, but it stayed there—with life-changing consequences.

When Maria found out JJ was a suspect, she rushed to the Bronx, picked up JJ, Vanessa, and her two grandsons, and drove them to a hotel in New Jersey to figure out what to do. By then they'd learned JJ was a suspect in the shooting of a former police officer, and over the weekend Maria searched for a lawyer, calling friends and asking if they knew anyone. On Sunday afternoon they finally got in touch with Franklin Gould, a veteran defense attorney, and he agreed to meet them Monday morning in front of the 28th Precinct in Harlem so that JJ could turn himself in.

On the way there the next day, Maria played a CD of the gospel song "Potter's Hand." The song is about giving your life over to the hand of the potter, to God, to be molded and taken care of. JJ remembers that the song calmed him, even if only temporarily.

Frank Gould was waiting for JJ at the precinct, and as his mother drove away, she watched as he and her son went inside. When she was a few blocks away, overcome with fear, she told me, she screamed.

Gould told JJ that he had spoken with detectives and found out that they had not yet secured an arrest warrant for him but wanted him to volunteer to appear in a lineup anyway. Gould advised against it, but JJ insisted he knew nothing about the crime and wanted to clear his name.

Detective Joseph LiTrenta conducted a lineup with JJ and five other men—"fillers," in police jargon—who all wore knit hats covering their hair. JJ was sitting in seat 2.

None of the fillers were light-skinned Black men. In a proper lineup, fillers should be selected who match the initial description of the perpetrator, not a particular suspect. In this case, all of the initial descriptions of the suspect were the same, a light-skinned Black man, but all the fillers were Hispanic.[1]

Witnesses Robert Jones, Phillip Jones, Dorothy Canady, Joe Scott, Lorenzo Woodford, and Augustus Brown all viewed the lineup from behind a one-way mirror.

Dorothy Canady told the police that she did not recognize anyone.

Joe Scott identified a filler.

Lorenzo Woodford asked both JJ and a filler to approach the one-way window. Woodford first identified number three, then immediately after that said, "Maybe number two," then finished by saying he "was not positive."

But Augustus Brown, Robert Jones, and Phillip Jones all identified JJ as the killer, and JJ was arrested for murder on the spot, even though he isn't Black, which is how all the eyewitnesses first described the gunman. In fact, on the mug shot that Augustus Brown first selected—the one that should have not been in the system—JJ's race was listed by police as "white Hispanic." But now that he was identified as the suspect in Al Ward's murder, Detective LiTrenta changed JJ's race to "Black Hispanic" on the new arrest booking photo.

By nightfall, the crumbling infrastructure and acute danger of Rikers Island had become JJ's new reality.

But soon, Maria felt hope. Shortly after she found out that the murder happened on January 27, she remembered that at the same time as the shooting JJ had been talking on the phone with her—proof, she believed, that her son couldn't have committed a murder.

There was a very specific reason why she and JJ remembered that call. JJ's father, whom he considered his best friend, had died nine months earlier, and January 28, the next day, was his dad's birthday, the first since his death. To honor him, JJ wanted his entire family to visit his grave site. But there was a problem: Maria and Vanessa had been fighting and weren't speaking.

On January 27, the day of the crime, JJ called his mother at her home in Haverstraw from his apartment in the Bronx to explain how important it was to him that they all be at the grave site together, even though there was tension. They talked for more than an hour, and ultimately Maria agreed to go, which they did the next day, only to find that the gates of the cemetery were locked.

In the weeks following JJ's arrest, Maria embarked on a relentless pursuit to get the phone records, and when they finally arrived, there was documented proof of a seventy-four-minute landline phone call from the Bronx to Haverstraw at the time of the robbery. If JJ and Maria had been on the phone then, there was no way he could have been involved with the crime. They were both relieved, confident those phone records would settle the matter.

I asked JJ if he knew any of the eyewitnesses. He said he didn't, that they were all strangers, but he did mention something that happened just before his trial began. While he was in a holding cell behind the courtroom, he said he saw a man in another holding cell staring at him and then blurting out, "They're making me do it!"

JJ said he realized who it was only once that man took the stand to testify. It was Augustus Brown, the prosecution's key eyewitness. I didn't know what to make of that story, or even if it was true. But I kept it in the back of my mind.

11   SOME TYPE OF GAME

ON OCTOBER 18, 1999, inside a courtroom at 100 Centre Street in downtown Manhattan, Judge Jeffrey Atlas called the case of *People vs. Jon-Adrian Velazquez* to order. It was nearly two years after his arrest, two years JJ had been incarcerated at Rikers Island. Now his fate would be decided by a jury of nine men and three women.

JJ's codefendant, Derry Daniels, wasn't in the courtroom. Months earlier, the prosecutor, Eugene Hurley, had made an offer to Daniels, who was facing life in prison if a jury convicted him: plead guilty in exchange for a twelve-year sentence. Daniels had taken the deal and had already been sent away. But from the day I met JJ, he was adamant that he had never met Derry Daniels. This claim sounded eerily familiar, and troubling given what I'd learned about David Lemus and Olmedo Hidalgo and the NYPD's erroneous theories in the Palladium case. If JJ and Daniels didn't know each other, what was the theory of the crime? Two strangers commit a robbery and murder together in broad daylight in one of the busiest areas of Harlem?

I scoured the thousands of documents I'd gotten from JJ and whatever the NYPD and Manhattan DA's office would provide, which wasn't much. As far as I could tell, police and prosecutors had never been able to find any connection between the two men. I couldn't find much in the way of paperwork or police notes about Derry Daniels. But I did have the transcript of the court hearing where he pleaded guilty, and it left me scratching my head.

In what's called a plea allocution, a defendant admits guilt to a judge in open court, providing details of his role in a crime. When Derry Daniels gave his plea allocution, Judge Atlas allowed the prosecutor, Eugene Hurley, to take the lead in questioning Daniels to determine if the plea was factual.

This was the part of their exchange, according to the court transcript, that dealt with JJ:

> HURLEY: Can you tell us what was your role and what was Mr. Velazquez's role?
>
> DERRY DANIELS: My role, I was duct-taping.
>
> HURLEY: What was Mr. Velazquez doing?
>
> DANIELS: His role was the gunman.
>
> HURLEY: And you two agreed to this plan together; is that correct?
>
> DANIELS: Yes.

And . . . that was about it. *Really?* I thought. *Nothing like: "How do you know each other? When did you meet? How did you hatch this plan?" or "You're pleading guilty. Let's make sure you're telling the truth"?*

Nope.

This was the first and only time that Daniels had ever said that JJ was his accomplice. He never explained their relationship, a motive, or how they planned or executed the crime, and there is no evidence he was ever asked about it. Daniels never even said JJ's name.

Prosecutor Hurley knew that both JJ and Daniels had said they didn't know each other, but at Daniels's plea allocution he never tried to get to the bottom of what had really happened.[1]

JJ was represented by Franklin Gould and Norman Reimer, two overworked but highly respected attorneys who had been appointed by the court because JJ no longer had the money to pay someone. By the time the trial began, the two lawyers had successfully convinced the DA to stop seeking the death penalty, so JJ was facing twenty-five years to life—a small victory, perhaps, but to JJ obviously an important one.

Hurley knew the jury needed to hear from the key eyewitness, Augustus Brown, the first person to connect JJ to the murder. At the time, Brown was facing drug charges in Pennsylvania and didn't want to testify. But Hurley had Brown taken into custody in Pennsylvania and transported to New York by detectives on what's called a material witness order six days before the trial began, to ensure he would appear.

On the stand, Brown identified JJ as the shooter, telling the jury he had seen him before and had "no doubt" about his identification. And even though his original signed statement says Brown described the shooter as a "light-skinned Black male," he denied using the word "Black."

On cross-examination, Gould wanted the jury to hear about the pressure and threats Brown said he faced for hours at the precinct when being questioned. The detectives, he said, were going to arrest him for being a part of the crime if he didn't pick someone out.

GOULD: Do they say to you, "Look, you can walk out of here. We're not going to arrest you. We're not going to charge you, but if you don't cooperate, you're going down," or words to that effect?

BROWN: Yes.

GOULD: Who said that?

BROWN: The officer that questioned me.

GOULD: And when in relation to the questioning did they give you that threat, the beginning, the middle, the end?

BROWN: The beginning.

GOULD: So from the beginning that was the threat that you had in that precinct. Is that correct?

BROWN: Yes.

Detective LiTrenta denied Brown's claims. Brown also testified about the ten bags of heroin he had had in his underwear, telling the jury that after he pointed to JJ's picture detectives let him keep the drugs and he was free to go.

After Brown testified, he was released from custody, and the Manhattan DA's office paid for his lodging and meals. While this frequently happens with witnesses, the idea that the DA had jailed Augustus Brown for a week and then gave him a hotel room and meals only after he testified was striking.

Witness number two, Robert Jones, who had been working the door at the illegal betting parlor, estimated having seen the shooter for about three or four minutes when he first came in, and for about five or six minutes during the robbery approximately an hour later. Like Augustus Brown, despite initially describing the gunman as "Black" in his signed statement two hours after the murder, Jones also testified that he had actually told the police something else. He said, for the first time, that the gunman was a light-skinned Puerto Rican.

When asked to identify the shooter in court, Jones said he was certain that JJ, who is Puerto Rican, was the killer.

Witness three was Phillip Jones, Robert's brother.

At the time of trial, Phillip was serving his own prison sentence for drug possession and had entered into an agreement with the Manhattan district attorney. For his "truthful" testimony, the DA would write a letter on Phillip's behalf to the parole board so they could take his cooperation into account when deciding if he should be released from prison.

According to the Innocence Project, incentivizing people to testify has been shown to be a contributing factor in wrongful convictions. For example, in one-fifth of nearly four hundred convictions overturned by DNA evidence, a jailhouse informant who'd received a deal was found to have lied.[2]

Two hours after Al Ward's murder, Phillip Jones signed a statement taken by police describing the shooter as being "male black, light skin, with red hair." At trial, he denied saying any of this and identified JJ as the killer.

The fourth witness was Lorenzo Woodford. Despite not identifying JJ at the lineup and first describing the gunman as "Black," who "might have had braids," Woodford later said he knew it was JJ but was too scared to pick him out at the lineup. On the stand, he positively identified JJ as the shooter.

On cross-examination, Woodford testified that in the weeks after the murder he established a relationship with LiTrenta, the lead detective, and supplied him with information about other criminal activity in the 28th Precinct. Woodford, who had been homeless, testified that the Manhattan DA's office had been keeping him in a motel and giving him lunch money prior to giving his testimony.

A fifth eyewitness called by prosecutors was Dorothy Canady, who was eighty-eight years old at the time of the trial. Canady hadn't identified JJ at the lineup, and shortly after he became a suspect, she pointed to two fillers as possibly the shooter when shown an array that included JJ's photograph. After meeting with the DA eleven days after the crime, she said she realized after leaving the lineup that the shooter was JJ.

But when prosecutor Hurley asked her to make an in-court identification of the perpetrator, this is what happened:

> HURLEY: I'd like you to look around the courtroom and tell us whether you see the fellow who had the gun in court right now?
>
> CANADY: The one with the white shirt on [*indicating*].
>
> HURLEY: Over here in the jury box?
>
> CANADY: Yes.
>
> HURLEY: I'd like you to look at the whole courtroom.
>
> GOULD: For the record.
>
> JUDGE: Yes, we have to make a record. Ma'am, you said the one with the white shirt on. Are you looking over to the right in the jury box, this group of people?
>
> CANADY: Right here.
>
> JUDGE: The fellow with the white shirt, indicating juror number six?
>
> CANADY: Yes.
>
> HURLEY: Ma'am, I'd like you to look around the whole courtroom, Miss Canady. I'd like you to look around the whole courtroom. [*Brief pause.*] And what's your answer?
>
> CANADY: Still say—
>
> HURLEY: Do you believe this person that's—
>
> CANADY: Yes.

I actually had to read this a few times, just to make sure I got it right. A witness had identified juror number 6 as the gunman, a Hispanic man with a bald head. When that happened, the courtroom erupted with laughter. JJ told me it's a moment he can never forget.

"The only two people who were serious were me and the prosecutor. The prosecutor's pissed off because she picked the wrong person, and I'm mad because everyone thinks this is a joke. This is my life."

After the prosecution rested, JJ said he was afraid but confident. He said even the court officers escorting him told him that he'd be going home.

It was now time for JJ's lawyers, Gould and Reimer, to present their case: not only was JJ the wrong man, but they could prove it.

Vanessa Cepero, the mother of JJ's sons, was the first defense witness called. She testified that she knew exactly where JJ was on January 27, 1998.

> **GOULD:** Where was he?
>
> **CEPERO:** He was home with me and the two kids.

Vanessa said she remembered JJ talking to his mother on the phone for a long time, and that she never spoke with Maria.

> **GOULD:** Now was there some particular reason why January 27, 1998, stuck out in your mind?
>
> **CEPERO:** Yes.
>
> **GOULD:** What was significant about that day?
>
> **CEPERO:** The following day would be his father's birthday.

Frank Gould then called Maria Velazquez to the stand. Maria testified that on January 27 she paged her son several times because she wanted to speak with him about the next day's arrangements to visit his father's grave site at the cemetery.

> **GOULD:** And did there come a time when he called you back?
>
> **MARIA:** Yes, he did.
>
> **GOULD:** And did you have a conversation with him?
>
> **MARIA:** Yes.
>
> **GOULD:** And about how long did that telephone conversation last?
>
> **MARIA:** Seventy-four minutes.

Maria said she never spoke with Vanessa during that conversation. The defense introduced their phone bill showing the call overlapping with the time the crime was happening.

Prosecutor Hurley attempted to refute this phone call by making Maria seem like just a mother simply trying to save her only child from prison.

HURLEY: Now, ma'am, you have no other children, correct?

MARIA: No, I do not.

HURLEY: And I assume that you want to be able to help your son, if you can, correct?

MARIA: Yes.

HURLEY: Thank you.

JJ also took the stand and testified on his own behalf, something that many people in his position don't do in order to avoid cross-examination. He told the jury he'd never been to Al Ward's numbers spot or any others, and he said he hadn't heard about the murder before becoming a suspect. He insisted that he was innocent.

Like Maria and Vanessa before him, JJ explained that he had been on the phone with his mother.

"Well, it was a tough time for me," he said. "There was a lot of things going on in the family as far as really concentrating on my mother and Vanessa. They weren't getting along. They weren't speaking to each other. My family is very important to me and the support from my family, of my children, is very important to me. The next day was my father's birthday. It was the first date, first birthday, that I would be experiencing without him because he passed away the year prior, and I was trying to make my mother and Vanessa realize how important it is for a family to be together at a time like that, and it was a long conversation."

On cross-examination, prosecutor Hurley attempted to refute the phone call by pointing out that JJ hadn't actually remembered it until he looked at the phone records.

HURLEY: Well, now you were testifying just a moment ago that the phone conversation with your mother was at 11:44 a.m., right?

JJ VELAZQUEZ: Yes, sir.

HURLEY: The reason that you know that time is because you read it on the phone record?

JJ VELAZQUEZ: Yes, sir.

HURLEY: You don't have an actual recollection about it, you read it on the phone record?

JJ VELAZQUEZ: I just know it was late morning, early afternoon.

JJ's defense attorney Frank Gould emphasized that JJ didn't match the description of the shooter. Every witness initially had said the shooter was Black, and most said he had braids. But Gould pointed out that JJ isn't Black and that he had testified he'd never had braids. The defense even produced a photograph of JJ and his family taken a few weeks before the crime, when his son Jacob was born. In that photo JJ had short hair and no braids.

There was something else significant about the identification. All of the witnesses were Black, and JJ isn't. Research has found when it comes to witness reliability, it's more likely that you will be misidentified by someone of a different race, and that both white and Black people are significantly more accurate identifying own-race faces than other-race faces.[3] But JJ's jury never learned that.

Gould also addressed the pressure put on witnesses to make an identification. Hurley objected, prompting a sidebar, where Gould told Judge Atlas out of earshot of the jury that the jurors had "the right to know the lengths [the police] went to before somebody was identified."

But Judge Atlas was not convinced. "We are not going to spend the rest of the day conducting an investigation of the police department."

In summation, the defense pointed out that with all the police-recovered forensic evidence from the scene, not a single item implicated JJ.

The prosecution argued that even if the eyewitnesses weren't all precise, it was "too much of a coincidence" they would all pick out the same man. And while Hurley never disputed the call happened, he suggested they were all lying to protect JJ, and that a man as old as JJ would never talk so long to his mother.

> HURLEY: The claim here is that a twenty-two-year-old man had a seventy-four-minute conversation with his mother. Now, this is not his girlfriend or his boyfriend. This is his mother, a seventy-four-minute conversation from a twenty-two-year-old man. I think that you'll admit, if you think about that, that that is a highly unlikely event. It just doesn't ring true—if you'll pardon the expression.

The jury got the case on the morning of October 26, 1999, a Tuesday, and deliberated for three days, during which time they remained sequestered at a hotel in Queens. Their verdict came late on Friday afternoon: JJ was acquitted on the top count of first-degree murder, but he was found guilty of second-degree murder and multiple counts of robbery.

As his mother, Maria, broke down behind him, JJ was immediately handcuffed and returned to Rikers Island, where he would spend the next five months waiting to be sentenced.

When I first heard that prosecutors said five eyewitnesses had identified JJ, I thought it sounded airtight. But after reading their testimony, it hardly sounded like a slam-dunk case anymore. The prosecution's evidence was basically a few shaky witnesses who changed their description of the shooter and got deals, and an elderly woman who identified a juror as the gunman.

And after reading the trial transcript, something else struck me as odd. The jury never learned about Derry Daniels, JJ's alleged coconspirator who had pleaded guilty, saying he and JJ committed the crime together. Even though Daniels pleaded guilty, his name barely came up at all during JJ's trial. Why wouldn't the DA call him to testify against JJ?

On March 7, 2000, JJ stood before Judge Jeffrey Atlas for the last time. The judge asked him if he had any final comments prior to hearing his sentence.

"In my eyes the justice system played some type of game," JJ said. "I can't understand why I'm still in this courtroom. I've served over two years in jail for a crime I did not commit. As God's witness, I had nothing to do with this crime." He concluded with these words: "For those who do look at it like it's some type of game, winners and losers, there will be no winners here. We are all losers. We have not found your killer yet. Instead, an innocent man will go on to serve a life sentence while the murderer remains at large. I sincerely hope one day you find your man."

Then Judge Atlas sentenced Jon-Adrian Velazquez to twenty-five years to life in prison. He was twenty-three years old.

12   THE CHALLENGE

THE FIRST COUPLE OF years JJ was locked up at Green Haven, he'd do what most of the other guys did in the prison yard: run laps, lift weights, talk nonsense. But one day some older guys who'd noticed that JJ seemed smart and composed encouraged him to get involved with some of the organizations run by the incarcerated men. They believed that it was important to "use your brain and be mindful," JJ recalled.

That changed everything for JJ.

He began to study and read. He formulated questions about his trial. Now that he had been convicted, his trial attorneys no longer represented him, and his new, court-appointed appellate lawyer largely ignored his pleas to visit. He realized that if he was ever going to get out, he was going to have to do it himself, and he would need his entire case file—which turned out to be excruciatingly frustrating to get from behind bars. It took two years before the files finally arrived in a sixty-six-pound box that barely fit under his bed.

"I spent days pulling out files," he told me later. "They were stacked everywhere, even on the cardboard I kept over the toilet. I fell asleep with paper on me. I woke up with paper all over the floor. I kept thinking, *This box has magical powers: there's something in here that's going to help me.*

It takes a lot of skill and patience to get anything done in prison, much less to reinvestigate a murder and unpack a criminal case. JJ began spending every second he could in the law library, combing through legal cases, teaching himself the language used to lock him up. He read through thousands of pages of documents. He filed FOIA (Freedom of Information Act) requests for public records. He made research calls from the phone in the yard, even in the sleet and snow, and essentially became a self-taught paralegal.

As he pored over every note and sheet of paper in that box, JJ noticed that

44 out of a total of 125 police reports had never been turned over to his attorneys during the discovery process, even though they had been requested.

He found a letter that Eugene Hurley, the prosecutor, had sent to his attorneys, dated two weeks before the trial began, telling them he had decided to withhold those reports because they were irrelevant to JJ's case. It made JJ wonder what those reports said and why Hurley hadn't turned them over.

Perhaps the bigger question is why JJ should have had to wonder what was in his own file in the first place, and why a prosecutor was the gatekeeper of potentially critical information. According to JJ's trial transcript, Hurley provided the defense with new information during lunch breaks as the trial was under way, giving them no time to investigate or even properly evaluate the evidence. This discovery issue has been a national focus of reform, and in 2019, New York passed a law giving criminal defendants a right to more information before their trial begins.[1]

The more new information JJ found inside that box, the more livid he became. "This file's contents have made me question the integrity of the prosecution as well as the police officers that conducted the investigation in this case," he wrote me just months after I first met him in 2002. "Some very important key facts never came to the surface during the trial. There was another suspect in this case. He was known to the Police Department and residents of that neighborhood as 'Mustafa.' He was the primary suspect in this case stated in the original report. He fits the description made by all of the witnesses."

I wondered how it was possible JJ had never heard about Mustafa before, because the name was all over the police reports. JJ's lawyers obviously had them too, because they were the ones who had sent him the sixty-six-pound brown box full of the paperwork he was reading.

When he learned about Mustafa, JJ was enraged. Whether a guy named Mustafa was involved or not, there seemed to be far more tips and information about this Mustafa than about JJ. If Mustafa, whoever or wherever he was, had done it, not only was JJ doing his time, but Mustafa had gotten away with murder, and he might still be dangerous.

A defense investigator should have learned whether Mustafa was a viable alternative suspect before JJ's trial. JJ told me he did have a private investigator assigned by the court but said he never did anything. "I never got an investigation," was among the first things JJ told me when we met.

I had trouble believing that was true, given the serious charges JJ had been facing. So I tracked down that investigator, David Barrett. He confirmed what JJ told me. Barrett explained that JJ's lawyers never asked him to do much of anything. He wasn't given a copy of the file to review, he wasn't provided with all the police reports, and he didn't remember being asked to look for an alternative suspect named Mustafa.

Barrett said that the only thing he'd done was make a single visit to the block where the crime happened, but he hadn't learned anything. He explained that in court-appointed cases the pay is low and the workload is enormous for both lawyers and investigators. The lack of resources devoted to adequately mounting a defense in JJ's case was typical, a routine failure of the judicial system.

I wanted to know what JJ's trial lawyers had to say about all this, especially because nearly everyone I spoke with in New York's legal community said Frank Gould, JJ's lead attorney, had a stellar reputation as a staunch advocate for his clients. When I got in touch with him a decade after the trial, he said he hardly remembered JJ or the case, but by the time I reached him, I'd been told Gould was suffering from dementia. He's since passed away.

Norman Reimer, JJ's other lawyer, wouldn't cooperate or do an on-the-record interview with me despite JJ's repeated requests that he do so, although he did say that he always believed JJ was innocent.

I was slowly learning the harsh reality of what it means to be charged with a serious crime when you don't have the resources to aggressively defend yourself. Obviously, JJ couldn't do any digging himself, so my work was clear: I'd have to give his case the investigation it should have gotten in the first place.

Since I'd first met him in 2002, JJ had been almost taunting me to do it. On more than one occasion he dared me to prove him guilty. "You can't," he said, "because I'm not." Finally, five years later, in 2007, two days after the Palladium story aired, I interviewed JJ on camera for the first time and told him I'd take him up on his challenge.

"I don't know what the truth is here," I told him, "but if I find out that you're innocent, I'll keep going. It might take ten years, fifteen years, but I'll keep going." I had no idea how long it really would take.

My bosses didn't know about JJ or that I was investigating another claim of a wrongful conviction. So while I spent most of my day job working on other stories, I tried to do something on JJ's case whenever I had a few hours to spare. I started my interviews with JJ's sons.

From the moment I looked into Jacob's sad eyes in that prison lobby on Thanksgiving morning in 2002, I had often wondered what life was like for him and his brother, Jon Jr., without their dad at home, regardless of JJ's guilt or innocence. Back then, the boys had been eight and five. Now it was 2008, and they were fourteen and eleven. Documenting their journey began to feel more important as JJ's letters became more personal and vulnerable. He wrote about how much he missed his sons and how concerned he was about Jon Jr. in particular. Now that he was a teenager, he was hanging out late, drinking, and blowing off school.

> I love my son, Dan! And my biggest fear throughout my entire incar-
> ceration has always been feeling helpless during the moments when my
> children need me the most. . . . How does a father sit idle while his chil-
> dren are clearly suffering? How can a father accept that there is nothing
> that he can do?? Is it all right for a father to trick himself into thinking
> that everything will be all right, even when matters are only getting
> worse??? I haven't told anyone this, Dan, but I've been waking up in the
> middle of the night worried about my son.

There is always collateral damage to imprisonment, including what's be-come known as "a cycle of incarceration." A child with a parent in prison has a higher chance of going to prison too. JJ knew this, had seen it happen to other families, and behind bars he felt powerless to keep that from happening to his sons. When he wrote to me about waking up in the middle of the night wor-ried that something bad was going to happen, was he predicting the future? I hoped not. But it was clear that JJ's incarceration was taking a toll on his family, and I thought documenting the journey of his boys, wherever it went, was a valuable thread in this story.

I went to visit them where they lived with their mother in the South Bronx. Their apartment building was across the street from a couple of burnt-out row houses. Jon Jr. said he knew that drugs were often sold back there, and he sometimes heard gunshots at night. He said he wanted to become an internal affairs officer for the NYPD one day to root out corrupt cops because of what happened to his dad, and because of what he'd experienced too, like the run-in he and some friends recently had with undercover police officers.

"We just all sitting on a bench and stuff, and a car pulls up and I hear doors open and then the doors slam. I get up and I start running, but I didn't know they was cops 'cause they're wearing all black. And then he takes me, and he slams me."

Jon Jr. said he thought he was being robbed. "I'm like, 'What do you want? You can have anything in my pocket.' He was like, 'Nah, I'm a cop,' and he pulls out his badge. I was like, 'Mister, I didn't know. I'm sorry.'" Jon Jr. finished by telling me, "I don't really trust cops."

JJ's sons had been going with their grandmother, Maria, to visit their dad nearly every weekend their entire lives. Now, as they were becoming teenagers, they started going less. It had been six months since Jon Jr. had been to Sing Sing.

"I don't like to see my dad in prison," he told me. "I don't really like to go up there anymore."

Who could blame him? But I found it profoundly sad. He struck me as an innocent kid whose innocence was coming to an end. He already knew way too much about law enforcement and prison.

His younger brother, Jacob, never spoke much. I probably heard his voice only a handful of times in those early years. One time is vivid, though. I was showing Jacob how a wireless microphone works, and I said I needed him to say something to test it. Jacob simply said: "I love my dad very much."

The same day, I interviewed their mom, Vanessa Cepero, on camera. She and JJ were no longer together. She said she had tried her best after he was sent away to keep their relationship alive, but life got too hard. She had two little babies. She had no income, and she was shuttling back and forth to the prison. Finally she couldn't take it anymore. She'd since found a new man and had another baby.

When I'd asked JJ about Vanessa moving on, he said he understood. "I don't blame her. She didn't know if I'd ever be home, she had two young kids, so she's doing what she's gotta do," he said. "I gotta do time."

It had been many years since Vanessa had spoken with JJ. She said she knew he was innocent because she'd seen him having that long phone conversation with his mom that morning. She was stunned when he was convicted.

Just like Janice Catala said about David Lemus in the Palladium, Vanessa said about JJ, "I couldn't believe it. I knew he was with me."

With both Vanessa and his mother, Maria, as alibi witnesses, it sounded like JJ had a pretty strong defense to me. But at his trial, Eugene Hurley, the prosecutor, had successfully argued to the jury that Vanessa was lying to cover for the father of her children, and that she was really the one on that long phone call with Maria that morning. I pushed her, asking if it was possible that she spoke with Maria even for a short time.

"I didn't get on the phone with her for even one second. Me and his mother weren't talking," she told me. "We never really got along. I had nothing to say to her and she had nothing to say to me."

After we spoke, I went along with Vanessa as she took the boys to get haircuts. In the barbershop I caught Jon Jr. looking in the mirror at a few new hairs growing on his teenage chin and thought, *Man. His dad isn't here to teach him how to shave.* One more loss in a string of countless losses.

From the beginning, JJ claimed he didn't know his codefendant, Derry Daniels, and had never even said a word to him. Despite my own questions about the shaky identifications and the fairness of JJ's trial, I knew that if there was a connection between JJ and Daniels, it would mean JJ was lying to me and I would be done. I had to find Daniels.

By 2011, Daniels had served his time and was back home. It wasn't easy to locate him, but I eventually dug up his address in Newark. No one was home when I went there, so I waited in my car and after a few hours I spotted him. When I approached him and tried to show him a picture of JJ and ask him a few questions, he made it extremely clear he didn't want to talk, even for a minute, and then slammed the door in my face. I found his aggression odd.

Why wouldn't he speak with me? If JJ was really his partner in crime, why wouldn't he want to help him?

But I thought the most important people for me to talk to were the eyewitnesses who testified that JJ was the shooter. They provided the evidence—the only evidence—that led to his conviction.

One of the witnesses, Lorenzo Woodford, turned out to be living in Hartford. I'd reached out to him a couple of times, but he wasn't interested in talking to me either. So, several months later, I tried again. This time I asked one of my NBC colleagues, Stefani Barber, to do the knocking on Woodford's door, and it worked. They spoke for an hour outside his apartment building, with Barber wearing a hidden camera the whole time.

Woodford told her he would never forget the day Al Ward was shot. He said he was in the back room of the numbers joint around noon buying heroin from Augustus Brown when suddenly two men barged in. "I heard someone say, 'Give it up, motherfucker!' And this guy stuck a gun in my face."

Woodford said Al Ward then pulled out his gun and fired, and all hell broke loose. "I heard all these shots—boom, boom, boom! Before I got a chance to even think, I jumped up and ran."

Woodford said he went across the street, shot up heroin, and watched the police arrive. A few days after the shooting, after Augustus Brown had picked out JJ's picture, Woodford was shown a lineup with JJ in it.

"I don't have no problem recognizing people," Woodford said. "The kid that I said did it, that's who did it. All right? I never saw no sketches. I never saw no pictures. I never made no descriptions of him. I went to a lineup and picked him out of the lineup."

Except here was the problem with Woodford's story: it wasn't true. According to police reports and his own trial testimony, Lorenzo Woodford *did* give the police a description of the suspect. He said the shooter was Black and had braids. And when he was brought in to look at a lineup, he didn't pick out JJ right away. JJ was number 2 in the lineup. But, according to police notes, Woodford first picked number 3, then said, "Maybe number two," finally saying, "I'm not positive." And he still didn't seem so positive when Stefani Barber spoke to him.

"If they don't believe he did it, let him go!" Woodford said. "I didn't turn him in. Somebody else turned him in. All right? They didn't just take my word for it, they had to have some kind of evidence."

In fact, there was not a single shred of physical or forensic evidence that linked JJ to the crime scene. Woodford and the other eyewitnesses were the only evidence detectives had. And the most important eyewitness was obvious: Augustus Brown, the drug dealer who first linked JJ to the crime, kicking off the whole chain of events.

I'd found out Brown was incarcerated in upstate New York, serving a sentence for forgery, but I didn't want to tell him that I was coming because I didn't want to give him the time to think of reasons not to talk to me.

I had a good relationship with the folks in the press office at the Department of Corrections, and I asked them if I could bring in my gear without telling Brown I was coming, and they said that sounded okay to them. With a couple of colleagues, I made the six-hour drive to Elmira Correctional Facility.

Once we were inside a conference room, corrections officers went and got Brown, but when I introduced myself and told him why I was there, he turned like he was about to go back to his cell.

"Hey, man, we just drove six hours to come and see you!" I said. "Please just talk to me for a moment. Just talk to us. Please, it's important."

He agreed to talk, but I immediately sensed he would never agree to go on camera, so I made a split-second decision. I took out a little camera that was in my pocket, hit the red button, and put it on the shelf behind him because I wanted to make sure to document whatever he said in case he later denied it.

After we started talking, Brown stayed for an hour. He told me about the day of the crime, how police found him two days after the shooting and took him to the precinct, and how they found ten bags of heroin in his underwear. Brown said they put the drugs on the table in front of him while they interrogated him.

"They was going to lock me up," Brown told me. "They were threatening to charge me with conspiracy to this, saying that I set this up, for them to come in and rob it. Then me having that on my record, a young Black man, I ain't got no job. I'm not in school or nothing."

He said they then sat him in front of a computer screen where they had him look at what seemed like an endless database of mug shots, pressuring him to pick someone out, using that "trawling" method, also sometimes referred to as "suspect shopping."

"Were they yelling at you?" I asked him.

"They were manhandling me in there," Brown replied. "I was tired, scared. You know what I mean? That's the main thing, I was scared. Like, I mean, I can't go to jail for something I didn't do."

After looking at more than eighteen hundred photos, Brown finally pointed to JJ's picture. When he did, he was allowed to go home with his drugs, uncharged. He said he picked JJ's picture because he thought he looked familiar, but then said something that sent shivers down my spine: he was certain he did not actually recognize JJ from the numbers joint that day.

By the time JJ went on trial, Brown was on parole and facing drug charges in Pennsylvania. He told me that he hadn't wanted to testify in JJ's case, but Eugene Hurley, the prosecutor, asked a judge to issue what's called a material witness order to compel Brown to take the stand. Two detectives picked up Brown in Scranton, put him in handcuffs, and drove him to Manhattan, where he was put in a jail cell for a week until he testified.

I remembered the story JJ had told me a couple of years earlier, when I asked him if he'd ever met Augustus Brown. He said he'd spoken with Brown only once, behind the courtroom, when Brown had blurted out, "They're making me do it!"

Brown said the story was true.

"What did that mean, 'They're making me do it'?" I asked him.

"Like they're forcing me," he said. "Like, it was either that or go to jail."

Speaking with Brown rocked me. He was the only reason JJ had become a suspect, and here he was telling me that he knew JJ was the wrong man. While the key witness putting someone in prison with false testimony might be vital information, it was not enough to command an hour on *Dateline*, so I still hadn't pitched JJ's story to my bosses.

And yet I knew I had a moral imperative not to keep what Augustus Brown told me to myself.

13   BOB AND CELIA

JUST A FEW MONTHS after my conversation with Augustus Brown, a changing of the guard was under way at the Manhattan district attorney's office for the first time in thirty-five years. In January 2010 Robert Morgenthau retired, and his handpicked successor, Cyrus Vance, was sworn in.

Vance had run in part on a pledge to create a Conviction Integrity Unit, also known as the CIU, that would review claims of wrongful convictions. Reading about his initiative on his website, I happened on a list of people on Vance's transition team and immediately recognized one of the names: Bob Gottlieb.

Bob is a former prosecutor and a longtime defense attorney who had worked on many high-profile cases, and I remembered that during the Palladium case years earlier, he had made a very short court appearance after he was appointed to represent C&C gang member Joey Pillot. So I gave Bob a call to get his thoughts about the DA's new unit and told him about JJ's case. I then sent him and his partner, Celia Gordon, some of JJ's paperwork. Several months later, after reading through it and visiting with JJ, they decided to represent him, pro bono.

Bob and Celia hired a private investigator while I kept my own investigation moving forward separate from theirs, except one time when their investigator and I decided to visit Robert Jones together so he didn't have to repeat his story twice.

Robert insisted that JJ was the gunman. But it sounded to me like he had had a little encouragement from the NYPD when he picked JJ out of the lineup, because he said he was told ahead of time by a detective that one of the men in the lineup was believed to be the killer. Multiple studies have shown that is exactly the opposite of what a witness should be told, which is that the perpetrator may or may not be in the lineup.[1]

Best practices also dictate that lineups should be double-blind, meaning the detective who conducts the lineup as well as the witnesses viewing it shouldn't know the identity of the suspect. Studies have shown that when an officer is aware of who the suspect is, there can be a tendency to subconsciously signal that to a witness.

Also, witnesses trying to be helpful will do their best to make an identification even when they're not sure, and will often choose someone who looks familiar enough to give them a flash of recognition, even if the real suspect's picture is not among the photos.[2] And once they've picked out a picture, they are likely to double down on that ID if that person is placed in a lineup. Most important, what studies have shown since JJ's conviction is that memory is often faulty, especially when someone is shown dozens, or even hundreds, of photographs.

For all these reasons, eyewitness misidentification has been found to be the leading cause of wrongful convictions, contributing to approximately 70 percent of known exonerations proven through DNA evidence.

My own doubts about Robert Jones's credibility were only deepened when he told me that he saw someone at JJ's trial who seemed to resemble the shooter more than JJ. It turned out to be JJ's half brother, who is five years younger than him.

"I've been living with this since the time I saw his brother in the court," he said, though no one, other than Robert, had ever suggested JJ's half brother had anything to do with the shooting.

For his part, Phillip Jones, Robert's brother, who was also a witness, signed an affidavit for Bob and Celia's investigator after their interview saying that he knew JJ wasn't the gunman. It seemed like a real breakthrough. I needed to find Phillip myself to confirm what he said. I'd heard he was living in a certain neighborhood in Far Rockaway, Queens, so with his affidavit in hand and with a hidden camera in my shirt buttonhole, I went there to look for him. A couple of hours later I finally found him walking on his street. Philip didn't want to talk outside, but he invited me in.

First I made sure the signature on the affidavit was his. Then I read it back to him:

On 1/27/98, I was present at 2335 8th Avenue and witnessed my friend Albert Ward get shot and killed. On 2/2/98, I viewed a lineup in which

I picked out an individual as being the shooter, but I was not sure. I told the police this was the guy and I was sure, but this was not the truth. I felt pressured because the police were threatening to arrest me and my brother Robert for stealing money that Albert dropped on the floor after being shot. I was arrested sometime after Albert Ward was killed, and two detectives came to visit me upstate in Groveland prison. The detectives told me they got the right guy and would help me get parole. I decided to testify at the trial because I felt pressured by the police. When I saw the defendant in court, I looked in his eyes and I knew I had picked out the wrong guy and the guy on trial I had never seen before.

Signed, Philip Jones

"That's all true?" I asked.

"That's all true," he replied.

I'd now spoken with the four eyewitnesses who had sworn under oath at JJ's trial that he was Al Ward's killer. Of those four, Augustus Brown had recanted. Philip Jones had recanted. Phillip's brother Robert Jones had said someone else looked more like the shooter. And Lorenzo Woodford's story didn't match the facts, not to mention that he hadn't identified JJ in the lineup the week of the crime. Then, of course, there was the prosecution's fifth eyewitness, Dorothy Canady, who had pointed to juror number 6 when asked to identify the shooter. She had passed away.

It was clear to me that the evidence that had sent JJ away was a lot weaker than it first sounded. But the jury had found JJ guilty, and I wanted to know why and how. So I decided to call juror number 6, the one picked out by Dorothy Canady as the gunman, and he agreed to an interview.

His name is Ramon Aviles, and I asked him a question that seemed obvious. How could he vote guilty when one of the witnesses had pointed to him in the jury box and picked him out as the shooter?

He said he'd done his best, that he'd tried to be as fair as he could and maintain an open mind, and that he and a few other jurors initially voted not guilty. But most of the other jurors were convinced JJ was guilty, and ultimately they convinced him and the other holdouts that JJ's girlfriend, Vanessa, seemed to be covering for him.

"It kept going back to the girlfriend. The witnesses were a cast of characters, and that didn't help. Once it came to Vanessa, in my opinion, that became the central point."

Aviles remembers the three-day deliberation was stressful and tense. Ultimately, he said, he felt pressured by the other jurors because it was late on a Friday and they were desperate to go home. But after the verdict was read, he said he felt like something terrible had happened. "Once it was announced," he said, "I looked at the mother, then I looked away. In other words, I didn't know where to put my face. I guess that's what I had to live with from that time on."

He said he immediately thought he'd made a mistake, and even went back to the courthouse to ask the clerk if he could take back his vote. He was told that was impossible.

It took JJ's lawyers, Bob Gottlieb and Celia Gordon, more than a year to conduct their own investigation, but everything they discovered only pointed to JJ's innocence. They were convinced of it, and they were optimistic that soon others would see it, too. JJ's case seemed like a perfect candidate for DA Cyrus Vance's new Conviction Integrity Unit, so they prepared a detailed submission for Bonnie Sard, who had been appointed by Vance to serve as the inaugural chief of the unit.

Sard had served as an assistant district attorney for over twenty-five years and was a member of Vance's executive staff. She later managed the internal operations of the office, including the vetting and hiring of approximately seventy-five ADAs each year from more than a thousand applicants.

In October 2011, Sard notified Bob and Celia that the CIU had decided to reinvestigate JJ's case and requested all the material they had, even their private investigator's recordings. All JJ could do was wait. But at least he felt new hope.

So did his mother. "In God we trust," Maria told me, "because men make mistakes."

When I first met JJ in 2002, I'd gone into my investigation skeptical of his innocence. By 2011, I was certain of it. And I wanted to get his story on the air.

I'm often asked how I know I have enough for a show, and I don't have an answer. Every story and situation is unique, but when it comes to wrongful convictions, there's a series of questions that usually helps me decide whether to move forward: Can I prove this person is innocent, and if so, how well can they tell their own story? Do I have the elements to be able to actually make it a television show? And if I do have those first two things, do my bosses even want it? If they don't, how do I get it done anyway?

In the end, what actually gets on TV is not up to me, and that was especially true about this story. I still had to convince a lot of people, including *Dateline*'s executive producers, David Corvo and Liz Cole, as well as an NBC lawyer, David Sternlicht. After all, JJ was a convicted cop-killer, and I was pushing to air a prime-time hour even more complicated than the Palladium story, where I followed a detective investigating an innocence claim. In JJ's case, it was my own investigation that was suggesting he was falsely incarcerated as a result of shoddy work—or something even worse—on the part of the NYPD and the Manhattan DA's office.

When I feel strongly about a story, I look for anything I can find that will make it feel special or different enough to get a green light from my bosses. For JJ, that difference came in the form of a young reporter named Luke Russert.

The idea had come to me when my Palladium documentary was nominated for an Emmy Award. We didn't win, but after the ceremony, I bumped into Luke, whose father was the beloved *Meet the Press* moderator Tim Russert, who had suddenly and tragically died of a heart attack three months earlier. Over that summer, Luke had been hired at NBC News. I asked him if he'd be interested in discussing the possibility of fronting JJ's story, pitching it partly about his journey as a young reporter investigating the case. He loved the idea and went to Steve Capus, the president of NBC News, saying he wanted to do it. And that's the reason JJ's story got a green light.

It can take a long time to produce an hour of television, especially a story like JJ's that is legally, editorially, and logistically complex. Not to mention that JJ's story wasn't exactly at the top of the *Dateline* priority list. There would be weeks or months when I would have to turn my attention to other projects. But by the end of 2011, the hour that we titled "Conviction" was ready for broadcast.

The show ended up finally running on Sunday, February 12, 2012. Despite going up against the Grammys on the same weekend Whitney Houston died, there was a huge response. JJ got mail from all over the world, and the show eventually got three Emmy nominations (though even with Luke in our corner we didn't win any).

The NYPD and the Manhattan DA's office wouldn't comment for the show. They offered no reaction to it after it aired, either. But I began to wonder if my name and address were being scribbled on prison bathroom walls, given the way my mailbox began filling up with pleas from incarcerated people from all over the country with claims of innocence. While I was well aware that many of those people were likely lying or mitigating their culpability, I was beginning to understand that wrongful convictions were far more common than I'd imagined.

JJ watched the show in the prison on a wall-mounted TV shared by the cell block. He told me: "I was happy. I was sad. I was confused. I went through a lot."

But he said the fact that the show aired gave him hope. He had received a lot of support from his fellow prisoners and piles of mail from people around the world, and he finally felt like he wasn't alone. For my part, I was confident that now that the truth was out, JJ's freedom was all but guaranteed. He did too, especially because he believed that people in the DA's office were finally paying attention and taking his claim of innocence seriously.

After JJ's story aired, other convicted men at Sing Sing began approaching him to say that they'd been railroaded as well. JJ knew that each case represented thousands of pages of paper and nuanced, complicated facts and that there was no way I'd have the time to look into them all on my own, so he said he would vet each case himself and only bring a claim to my attention if he thought there was merit to it.

In June, four months after my *Dateline* show, I visited JJ to get a sense of how he was holding up. Instead, I learned there were clearly more secrets behind the walls of Sing Sing.

"I have someone else," JJ told me.

"Really?" I said. "You gotta be kidding me."

"Really. His name is Eric Glisson."

A couple of days later, I was back in Sing Sing's visiting room, listening to Eric's terrible story.

14   ERIC GLISSON AND THE BRONX SIX

I WENT TO VISIT Eric Glisson at the end of June 2012. As we spoke for hours in Sing Sing's visiting room, Eric struck me as a friendly, sweet-tempered man with a high-pitched voice and easy smile who was eager to share with me the nightmare he'd been living for nearly eighteen years.

Eric said he was one of *six* people who had been wrongfully convicted of murder and sent to prison. How could six people who mostly didn't know each other be convicted together? If Eric was telling the truth, his story was the most outrageous one, at that point, that I'd ever heard.

Eric said that it all started on February 3, 1995. He was at home alone in the South Bronx when police burst through his door and arrested him. Just one week earlier, he'd become a father.

He was taken to the 43rd Precinct, where, for some reason, an assistant district attorney instead of a detective began to question him about the murder of a livery cabdriver a couple of weeks earlier. Eric insisted he knew nothing about it. I later got hold of the videotape of Eric's interrogation, which seemed to me an obvious attempt to intimidate a scared and vulnerable young man. Sitting in a chair, bent at the waist, his voice breaking and his hands shaking, Eric frantically denied knowing anything about the murder. When he was told it had taken place in the early hours of the morning, Eric said he never would have been out in the middle of the night; he had a new baby and he was always home by ten thirty. As he pleaded and wept, he kept insisting that they should go look for the real killer. He was beside himself.

"I didn't do nothing!" he kept saying again and again. "Please, I just want to see my daughter! Please!"

During the summer of 2012 I made several trips to Sing Sing to film interviews with Eric, and I read thousands of pages of police reports and trial transcripts learning the details of his case.

The murder for which Eric was convicted had taken place seventeen years earlier on the morning of January 19, 1995, when Baithe Diop, a forty-three-year-old Senegalese immigrant working as a livery cabdriver to support his six kids, was found slumped over his steering wheel in the Soundview section of the South Bronx, shot multiple times, the victim of an apparent robbery.

The police investigation was run by a rookie detective named Mike Donnelly, working on only his second murder case. This was the same Mike Donnelly whom I had recorded in 2002 chiding former detective Bobby Addolorato for his Palladium obsession.

A team of police officers knocked on hundreds of doors in the area, asking if anyone saw or heard what happened. Only two people said they had, and both told police the same story: they could not identify the shooters, but after hearing gunfire they did see one or two men running from the scene.

Donnelly hatched his own theory of the case: whoever ordered the cab was probably involved with the murder. So he interviewed the dispatcher who took the call. The dispatcher said she believed the caller was a regular customer whom she knew as "Yvette," and that she would be able to recognize her voice if or when she called again. Donnelly told the dispatcher that if she did, she should tell "Yvette" that he wanted to speak with her.

Four blocks away, on the same night as the Diop murder, Denise Raymond, a thirty-nine-year-old executive at FedEx, had been found in her apartment shot twice in the head, with three pairs of handcuffs on her wrists and a sock stuffed into her mouth. Detective Thomas Aiello, a veteran just weeks away from retirement and a mentor of Donnelly's, was handling the Raymond case.

The big break came in the livery cab investigation two weeks later—or so Donnelly claimed—when a teenager was arrested for drug possession and told police he lived across the street from where Diop was killed and had information about the crime. The teenager said a woman named Miriam Tavares—a drug addict and prostitute who lived in the neighborhood and often slept on his family's couch—told him she'd witnessed the shooting.

Donnelly went to the teenager's home to speak with Tavares, but he had to ask the boy's sixteen-year-old sister, Cathy Gomez, to translate because Donnelly spoke only English and Tavares spoke only Spanish. Tavares told Donnelly that she had witnessed the crime looking through her bathroom window, knew who the shooters were, heard what they said, and saw what they stole. She gave Donnelly the names of five young men from the neighborhood, one of whom was Eric Glisson, whom she had once had a sexual encounter with.

But by the time Detective Donnelly left the apartment, he also had a signed statement from someone else: Cathy Gomez. Although she had only been asked to serve as a translator, Donnelly said she was also a witness in the Denise Raymond case. Donnelly claimed that Gomez told him that a couple of days before both killings she was in one of the suspects' homes and overheard a conversation about the murder scene and "robbing a taxi and a girl."

Based solely on the statements of Tavares and Gomez, all five men, including Eric Glisson, were arrested, charged with both murders, and sent to Rikers Island to await trial.

But Donnelly was still convinced that whoever called that cab must also have been involved. A few days after the shooting, a woman named Cathy Watkins called the livery car service and ordered a cab. Believing Watkins's voice to be that of "Yvette," the dispatcher told Watkins that a detective wanted to speak with her. Watkins dutifully called police to ask why, and they requested that she come into the precinct, so she voluntarily did.

While she was there, Donnelly asked Watkins to place a call to the dispatcher and pretend to order a cab, at one point yelling at her that she was trying to talk in a different voice. But the dispatcher, who was in an office down the hall in the precinct, said she recognized Watkins as the woman who called the night of the murder. Watkins was put in a lineup and Miriam Tavares identified her as being at the scene of the taxi driver's murder, saying she was directing the suspects by "snapping her fingers"—meaning to hurry and finish the robbery. Until then Tavares had never mentioned a woman being involved.

Based solely on Tavares's identification—and despite the fact that phone records indicated that Watkins did not in fact call the car service the night of the crime—Watkins was arrested for both homicides because the police's theory was that the same group had conspired to commit both murders. Watkins had no connection to the neighborhood or to the other suspects. But now she rounded out a group that would become known as the "Bronx Six."

Soon there would actually be a seventh defendant charged in Denise Raymond's case: her former boyfriend Charles McKinnon. Based on a single shoddy identification from a coworker saying she'd seen Raymond leave work with McKinnon the day of her murder, he was arrested.

With a total of seven defendants, the Bronx district attorney's office held three separate trials. McKinnon was acquitted of the murder of his former girlfriend, but the trial took a toll. He died five years later from heart failure, and his wife told me she believed that the stress of being falsely charged with murder had killed him.

As for the Bronx Six, there would be two trials. By the time they began, prosecutors had dropped charges against Eric Glisson and Cathy Watkins in the Denise Raymond case, citing lack of evidence. But they were tried together for the livery cab murder despite both insisting they had never met, and without a single piece of evidence that they ever had.

It was the same claim made by David Lemus and JJ in their cases, and with the same result: neither the police nor the prosecutors believed them.

Miriam Tavares was the sole incriminating witness in the taxi case, testifying that when she looked through her bathroom window she clearly saw six people kill Baithe Diop.

I got my hands on the NYPD crime scene video from that night, so I knew exactly where the cab came to rest after Diop was shot, and I went to the neighborhood to see for myself how Miriam's story matched up. As soon as I saw where her bathroom window was, I knew she'd been lying. The murder happened at least a hundred yards away, and at an angle that would have made it impossible for her to see what she said she had. I'd later learn that Detective Donnelly had never done that test himself. (I wanted to speak with Miriam Tavares, but she'd died of a drug overdose in 2002.) But based solely on Miriam Tavares's testimony, Eric Glisson and Cathy Watkins were convicted and sentenced to twenty-five years to life.

The remaining four of the Bronx Six—Devon Ayers, Michael Cosme, Carlos Perez, and Israel Vasquez—were tried together for both the FedEx executive and cabdriver murders. There were twenty-seven fingerprints recovered from Denise Raymond's apartment, and not a single one matched any of the accused men. Not a shred of forensic or physical evidence linked any of them to Diop's killing either. The key evidence in that trial was the testimony of Miriam Tavares and Cathy Gomez.

Three of the defendants were found guilty of both murders; Israel Vasquez was convicted of only Diop's killing.

The more I learned, the more incredulous I became. How could a jury have found so many people guilty on such a thin basis in fact? I'm still amazed that it could have happened. But it did.

After meeting Eric, I couldn't really grasp how he remained so good-natured given what appeared to be an appalling miscarriage of justice and his description of his experience in prison living in constant fear and suffering from crushing loneliness.

"They send you upstate, when you get on that bus, and they take you seven hours away and put you inside a cell," he told me, which he called "a living hell."

"The second day I'm there I see two Jamaican guys in the yard pulling each other's dreadlocks and stabbing each other up. Two weeks after that, I saw a guy get raped in the shower. The guy is screaming. And no officers come. After, he started wiping himself and there was blood on the tissue. My heart jumped. I thought that might be my fate. From that time on, I was in a state of complete shock."

He'd seen men try to hang themselves. He said that he understood that level of despair.

"You start to develop a sense of hopelessness, man, as each day goes by," he said.

Eric was eventually transferred to Sing Sing, and as the years passed, he tried to make the best of his prison life, immersing himself in the prison's programs in an effort to give himself a sense of purpose and keep busy. He became known as Sing Sing's MacGyver, someone who could fix anything. Once, he took apart two Walkmans and made a walkie-talkie. He also wrote his own scripts for TV commercials, one for sneakers with the tagline "Reebok till you drop. Just bokin'." And he vowed to fight for his exoneration. His mantra: "I die on my feet, not on my knees."

That meant finding the real killers from behind bars. He spent countless hours in the prison's law library, wrote hundreds of letters, and filed dozens of FOIA requests. He never got much traction, especially because he didn't have a lawyer. But help came from an unlikely person at the prison: a short Chinese-born nun named Sister Joanna Chan, a volunteer with a program called Rehabilitation Through the Arts, a group that puts on theater productions in prisons.

Eric formed a close relationship with Sister Joanna and began calling her "Grandma." One day they had just finished having a lunch of canned octopus during a break from play rehearsal when Glisson got some bad news. Grandma noticed he was upset and asked what was wrong. Eric explained that he'd just learned a federal court had denied his latest appeal.

Grandma said she wanted to help. She knew only one lawyer, named Peter Cross, who did corporate law and had never represented anyone convicted of a crime, but she got in touch with him anyway. After reading a little about the case and meeting Eric, Cross agreed to represent him pro bono.

Eventually Cross spoke with Cathy Gomez, who had been sixteen when she was asked by Detective Donnelly to serve as a translator. Cross was stunned by what he heard. Gomez, now thirty-three, explained that by the time she was done translating for Donnelly the night he came to her home, she had become the key witness in the investigation of Denise Raymond's murder by signing a sworn statement that she had overheard the same suspects talking about details of both crimes. But Gomez said Donnelly had coached her on what to say, and that she'd even told him, "I didn't see anything like that."

Still, she said, Donnelly had insisted she sign the statement, which she did without reading it, and she said she was later threatened with arrest if she didn't testify in the Raymond trial. Court transcripts show she'd even attempted suicide as the trial began.

So many lives ruined, and for what? As I looked at the case, all I could see were bumbling cops hell-bent on making arrests as quickly as possible.

But the NYPD was so proud of Detectives Donnelly and Aiello's work that in 1995, five months after the arrests, it had allowed the detectives to be featured in a glossy article in *New York* magazine titled "How to Solve a Murder:

Two Bodies, Few Clues: The On-the-Job Education of a New NYPD Detective by a Veteran in His Final Days Before Retirement."[1]

The story explained how Aiello taught the younger cop how to investigate a murder, and he offered assessments like "Sometimes hard work pays off. Sometimes it's luck." The older detective retired saying he was confident that justice in the Bronx Six case was being served.

15   THE LETTER

ERIC GLISSON KNEW HE had to take matters into his own hands to have any chance of getting another day in court. Like JJ, he fought to get every possible bit of paperwork related to his case. He never stopped his efforts, and every day he wrote pleading letters that began: "I am Eric Glisson and I am innocent." Nearly all of those letters fell into a void.

Then one day in early 2012, Eric received something through a FOIA request that he'd never seen before: a bill for the cabdriver's stolen cellphone showing that calls were made on the phone minutes after his death. From his prison cell Eric was able to track those last calls to associates of Gilbert Vega, who Eric learned was a member of a Bronx gang called Sex Money Murder. He also received a police report that had Gilbert Vega's name on it, indicating he'd been an early suspect.

On April 11, 2012, two months before I met him, Eric wrote yet another letter. This time he addressed it to a gang prosecutor in the US attorney's office, whom he figured would know the most about Sex Money Murder. But the gang prosecutor to whom Eric sent the letter had left the office. The woman who screened the mail easily could have tossed Eric's letter into the garbage. But a few years earlier another gang investigator had told her, "Listen, if anything comes in about any murders, just put it on my desk, okay?" And that's exactly what she did.

Like a miracle, that investigator was none other than John O'Malley, the same person who'd brought critical information to bear on the Palladium case. When O'Malley read Eric's letter, he jumped up from his desk.

After a twenty-year career as a detective in the Bronx and now in the US attorney's office, O'Malley was a bit of a savant when it came to details of gang murders in New York. He could tell you gang members' nicknames, who killed whom, where, when, and even why.

In the early 2000s, O'Malley had been investigating Sex Money Murder with a Bronx detective named Pete Forcelli and they would arrest a number of Sex Money Murder members, one of whom was Gilbert Vega. Like Joey Pillot had done years earlier in the Palladium case, Vega eventually flipped and became a cooperating witness who had to submit to one of those lengthy proffer sessions and admit to every crime he'd committed.

During one of those sessions in March 2003, Vega confessed to a crime O'Malley and Forcelli hadn't known about. Vega said that he and his fellow gang member Jose Rodriguez, known as "Joey Green Eyes," robbed and shot a livery cabdriver at Croes Avenue and Lafayette in the Soundview section of the Bronx.

Vega gave specific details, including how he and Rodriguez fled the car, then saw it roll down the street and crash. In an effort to corroborate his story, O'Malley visited Jose Rodriguez in federal prison, and Rodriguez admitted to the crime, confirming all the details Vega had given O'Malley and Detective Forcelli.

O'Malley called the 43rd Precinct—"multiple times," he'd later swear in an affidavit—and described the details of the crime. Each time he was told there was no record of a cabdriver being killed in 1995 in that area. O'Malley kept trying to find a police report or any documents related to the murder, but he came up empty.

Detective Pete Forcelli also tried, twice visiting the 43rd Precinct expecting them to have a cold case about a dead cabdriver, only to be told they had no case like that.

Like Forcelli, O'Malley had taken the NYPD's word for it and let it go. They knew that Vega and Rodriguez hadn't made up the story, but without proof of a murder, with no body or even a name of a victim, there was no homicide to admit to. Still, Vega and Rodriguez ended up pleading guilty in federal court to the shooting, not for murder but for discharging a firearm during the commission of a robbery.

Standing before a federal judge during Rodriguez's sentencing in January 2008, an assistant US attorney told a judge, "Mr. Rodriguez believed that the livery cabdriver was shot and killed. The government has not been able to find any record of a livery cabdriver being killed in a robbery."

"Well, I hope the man didn't die," said the judge.

"We have not identified that victim," the prosecutor continued. "We do know, based on Mr. Rodriguez's information plus the information from other sources, that there was such a robbery, there was such a shooting, but we've not been able to find a victim of a murder on that date."

What none of them knew until that letter from Eric Glisson landed on John O'Malley's desk in 2012 was that six people had already been convicted of the same crime nearly a decade earlier. O'Malley instantly realized it was the same crime that Gilbert Vega and Jose Rodriguez had confessed to years earlier, a crime for which the NYPD had told him there was no record. A shooting the men had even pleaded guilty to in federal court.

But O'Malley wanted to make sure he was right. First he arranged to speak to Vega again, and Vega repeated the same story. Then O'Malley drove up to Sing Sing to see Eric Glisson, who had no idea he was about to get a visitor.

"Who the fuck are you?" Eric said, with all the bluster he could manage.

O'Malley held up the letter and asked, "Did you write this?"

"Yeah, yeah, yeah, I wrote the letter," Eric said, his demeanor radically changed.

O'Malley shook Eric's hand and said, "I'm sorry. I know you didn't do this murder."

Eric's knees buckled, and he wondered if he was dreaming.

"I know you didn't," O'Malley said, "because I know the guys that did this murder. I'm not going to get into it with you here. But we're going to get you out of here. You have a lawyer?"

"Yeah," he said.

"Give me the lawyer's name and number," O'Malley said. "I promise you, when I leave this prison, I will call him."

He called Peter Cross as soon as he left the prison and was greeted with the same skepticism as had come from Glisson.

"Why are you meeting him?" Cross, who was standing in line at his bank, said. "I should have been present if there was something—"

"No, it's not like that. Listen to me: I know he didn't do it. I know who the murderers are, and it wasn't Eric."

There was silence on the phone. It had been six long years, and in front of a bank teller, Peter Cross's eyes filled with tears.

Margaret Garnett was John O'Malley's boss in the US attorney's office and the person he turned to when he found out about Glisson. Three days after meeting with Glisson, O'Malley and Garnett called Edward Talty, the chief of homicide at the Bronx district attorney's office, and informed him that Glisson had been convicted of a murder in which he had no involvement.

Talty told them that the assistant DA who had prosecuted the case, Daniel McCarthy, had recently died, and asked for time to gather the files and look into the case further. A couple of weeks later Garnett and O'Malley met with Talty, and O'Malley laid out the case, explaining how members of the Sex Money Murder gang were the real killers. But it did not go well.

Walking out of the building, O'Malley turned to his boss and said, "Margaret, that was like a 'Don't let the door hit you in the ass.' They don't believe us."

Understandably, Eric also thought after meeting with O'Malley that his freedom would come soon. But getting out wouldn't be easy.

In the fall of 2012, five months after John O'Malley's visit and five months after I first met Eric, I was back in Sing Sing to film an update with JJ. On my way out, I got permission to stop by Eric's cell.

With my camera rolling, an officer escorted me down A-Block's long corridor. Eric's cell was toward the end.

"Glisson, on your feet!" the guard ordered.

"Yes, officer!" he called back, leaping to attention.

Eric was surprised to see me, and seemed stressed, which I certainly understood. Knowing the details, and especially given O'Malley's involvement, I thought it was obvious he was innocent—and that the people in power had to know the same thing. Yet here he remained.

"Want to see what it's like to live in here? I can touch both walls," he said, holding his arms out to show how small his cell was. The summer had been sweltering, he said, and to cool off, he would sometimes lie on the concrete floor and put his feet in the toilet.

He was in agony, unsure of what was going to happen next.

"Why am I still here?" he asked me.

I looked through the bars into his tiny cell and saw his wall of newspaper clippings about his case and the cases of other wrongfully convicted people who'd been freed. But what Eric called his "wall of hope" wasn't providing him with much in the way of solace now.

Even before that visit, I felt a responsibility to do something. A couple of months earlier, I'd convinced WNBC in New York to cover Eric's case, using some of the video I'd shot of him.

"You're hoping and praying that they will realize their mistake," Eric said in the piece. "You're waiting for this guard to come and open up that gate and tell you, 'We made a mistake. You're free to go home.'"

Peter Cross was also interviewed and talked about Eric's daughter and what it meant for her to have her father in prison all those years. "She had to go to school and grow up with family and friends thinking maybe her dad's a murderer," he said. "He knew he wasn't, but what could he do about it?"

That made it all the more galling that he was still inside, still suffering, and still in danger.

But in October, two months after the WNBC story aired, Peter Cross got a call from Bronx assistant district attorney Ed Talty, who said he was ready to make a deal. Peter went up to Sing Sing to tell Eric the news in person, as my colleague Tommy Nguyen recorded Eric's reaction in the same small conference room where I'd interviewed JJ and Eric several times before.

Eric didn't know Peter was coming to visit. He'd been in the yard working out, and came into the room out of breath. Peter got right to it. "I spoke with Ed Talty today. The DA's office is now prepared to give you a conditional release."

Eric looked like he was about to pass out. "Today?" he asked, even more out of breath than when he'd first walked in.

"Not today," Peter said. "It's going to take a couple of more weeks. Here's the thing: they want you to wear an ankle bracelet for ninety days while they continue to investigate."

Investigate what? I thought. *Why can't they just admit they were wrong?*

"Well, if that's the condition of my release, that's fine," Eric said, almost like he was in a dream. "It hasn't set in yet," he said seconds later. "All the fighting that we've done over these years. I don't know what to say right now."

Eric Glisson was transferred to Rikers Island while he waited to see a judge.

On October 24, 2012, Eric walked into a courtroom with Cathy Watkins, the codefendant he'd still never met. Seventeen years after their convictions, they stood side by side in front of state supreme court justice Denis Boyle.

I had visited Cathy once at the Bedford Hills Correctional Facility a few months before and was taken by her intelligence, composure, and resilience in the face of the hell she'd endured. She was an innocent woman stolen from her life and her young daughter based on manufactured evidence. Yet, like Eric, she'd grabbed every opportunity in prison to grow, learn, and assert her humanity. She took classes and, in 2009, earned a bachelor's degree in sociology, even serving as class valedictorian and speaker during the commencement ceremony. I would have loved to visit Cathy more and interview her on camera, but she wanted no part of the story. Who could blame her?

Judge Boyle told Eric and Cathy that they were being released and confirmed that they would have to wear ankle bracelets for monitoring while the Bronx DA decided how to move forward. A few months later the DA agreed to vacate their convictions, and in January 2013 the rest of the Bronx Six were released, without ankle bracelets, putting an end to one of the most outrageous cases of false imprisonment in New York City's history.

When Eric was released from prison, I spent his first day of freedom with him. We ate at a restaurant in Greenwich Village, where he wolfed down his first non-prison meal in all those years—lamb chops—and I watched as he was introduced to a world drastically different from the one he had left behind two decades earlier. He was given a cellphone to talk to his family, but he didn't know how it worked; at first he held it upside down. He marveled over the twenty-inch TV screen in his hotel room: "It's the biggest TV I ever saw!" And he couldn't get over how he didn't need a key to get into his room: "I've got a hotel key that's *a plastic card*!" He called me into the bathroom, marveling how much nicer it was than "the amenities they had in prison," meaning the steel toilet located next to his head.

And on that first night of freedom, I watched him sink into a plush king-sized bed with cool white sheets while the eleven o'clock news was showing a story about his release. "I know my friends in Sing Sing are watching this and are happy for me," he told me, "but it's hard for me because JJ is still in there."

He finally got to spend time outside of prison with his daughter. And, wearing his ankle bracelet, Eric received his long-awaited degree from Mercy College, striding across the stage like he was walking on air.

He was still wearing that ankle bracelet when Hurricane Sandy hit. He was staying at an apartment in the West Village that Peter Cross's assistant, Charmaine, had found for him when the power went out and a low-battery alarm on the bracelet started going off. He called me from a police precinct where he'd gone to make sure they knew he wasn't trying to escape.

He sat there at the station and charged his bracelet until four in the morning. Somehow Eric managed to laugh about it, though to this day he wonders why Detectives Donnelly and Aiello and the prosecutors in the Bronx district attorney's office have never apologized or been punished.

The *Dateline* story we aired about Eric's case was called "A Bronx Tale," reported by Josh Mankiewicz, a *Dateline* correspondent and dear friend. Our broadcast would be nominated for four Emmy Awards, the most nominations for a single story of any network that year. Eric and Peter Cross were my guests at the ceremony. We didn't win an Emmy, but honestly, it didn't matter. My real Emmy was Eric. Today, more than a decade later, he is like a brother to me.

THE FAILURE OF THE CIU

CYRUS VANCE IS BEST known by most New Yorkers as the prosecutor who succeeded legendary Manhattan district attorney Robert Morgenthau, and for prosecuting high-profile defendants like Harvey Weinstein and Dominique Strauss-Kahn. But to many who do wrongful conviction work, he's also known for reneging on his promise to create an objective and collaborative Conviction Integrity Unit in New York.

The unit was supposed to be based on the model of the first CIU, established in Dallas in 2007 by the district attorney at the time, Craig Watkins. Watkins's simple acknowledgment that mistakes *might* have been made by his office was a bold, public admission that wrongful convictions can and do happen, and it underscored the urgency of addressing such a pressing issue.

Because of the tireless work of advocates and the advent of more sophisticated forensics, particularly DNA testing, more CIUs were created to be the vanguard of a new era of scrutiny, by addressing the inherent human fallibility of the people who make up "the system." By 2024, there were about eighty-five CIUs nationwide, all allegedly serving a noble purpose and as a testament to our unyielding pursuit of justice.

The burgeoning landscape of CIUs cannot be fully appreciated without also acknowledging the pivotal influence of Barry Scheck and Peter Neufeld, cofounders of the Innocence Project, which was established in 1992 and which has made it its mission to exonerate the wrongfully convicted and to advocate for reforms to prevent future injustices. Not only did the Innocence Project lead to exposing the stark reality of wrongful convictions, but it also offered a blueprint for CIUs to provide a structured approach to uncovering and rectifying legal mistakes.

In fact, DA Vance chose Barry Scheck to be among the people who helped him create Manhattan's first CIU, but Barry and many others grew increasingly disappointed with how that CIU seemed to be operating.

In 2011, when JJ Velazquez's lawyers, Bob Gottlieb and Celia Gordon, first approached Bonnie Sard, chief of the Manhattan DA's CIU, they took it as a good sign when she invited them to a meeting within days to discuss JJ's case. Based on everything they'd heard about the CIU's mission and all the new material they had pointing to JJ's innocence, they felt confident that a quick review could lead to vacating his conviction, saving him years of filing appeals. In fact, Bob and Celia told me Sard had even suggested that they wait to file an appeal until her unit could review the case.

A sign that things might not be as objective and speedy as they were promised was when JJ's lawyers walked into that first meeting. Sitting at the table, along with Sard and others, was someone Bob and Celia hadn't expected to see that day: Eugene Hurley, the very prosecutor who'd put JJ away in the first place.

"The prosecutor who tried JJ, who vouched for the shaky eyewitness, and who should be investigated himself should not have been in that meeting," Bob later told me. "That was wrong."

And any psychologist could tell you why: it's not a stretch to believe that Hurley would have every incentive to defend his own reputation rather than seek the truth. But Sard insisted that her investigation would be fair and thorough. It just wouldn't be quick.

Another year passed. Celia and Bob suggested that if Sard and her team would just interview JJ, they'd see that he was innocent. And their request was granted.

On October 3, 2012, two detectives picked up JJ from Sing Sing and drove him to the Manhattan DA's office. It was the first time in fifteen years that JJ had seen the streets of New York, the first time he'd been able to wear regular clothes, a white button-down shirt and khakis, instead of his prison greens. And he was on his way to appear before a team of lawyers whose job it was to investigate allegations of prosecutorial misconduct and mistakes in the criminal justice system.

"It was an amazing experience," he told me at the time. "Besides seeing bars and barbed-wire fences and walls, I was able to see cars and people that weren't dressed in green or blue. I felt free!"

The feeling didn't last.

JJ was brought to a conference room where his lawyers and three people from the CIU were waiting. His handcuffs were removed, and he took a seat at the head of the table. The interview was videotaped.

The first thing the prosecutors did was to have JJ walk them through what he had been doing the day of Al Ward's murder. He recounted the same story he had since the beginning, about being at home in the Bronx, the seventy-four-minute phone call with his mother regarding his father's birthday, how he eventually turned himself in because he had nothing to hide, and that he didn't know his codefendant.

But what the prosecutors seemed particularly interested in was pushing JJ for details about who his friends were in the 1990s and his time selling drugs on the street in Manhattan. Celia called me later that day to report what she'd witnessed.

"The line of questioning was so far afield of the murder case and why we thought we were there," Celia said. "It was clear that they were not interested in the truth."

At one point the prosecutors even asked about me: "So, this all started with Dan Slepian?" Then they wanted to know if I was paying JJ's legal fees. I wasn't. There were no legal fees. Bob and Celia were working for free.

The meeting lasted three and a half hours. When it was over, JJ was put back in handcuffs and driven back to Sing Sing. He called to let me know how it had gone.

"They had no interest in whether I was innocent or guilty," JJ said, sounding disgusted. "I came down there to talk about my innocence, and they started asking me questions about who did what in the nineties. They wanted me to give them information about other crimes. Is this a joke?"

The hostility coming from the DA's office was palpable. In court one day I'd seen Bonnie Sard in person for the first time. I went up to her and simply tried to introduce myself, but she walked right past me, flashing her palm in my face.

Later a source sent me an email Sard had written, from her Manhattan DA email address to an assistant US attorney, saying, "There's an investigative producer named Dan Slepian looking into this case. Here are his phone numbers. Does he show up in any of your investigations?"[1]

All those years ago in the Palladium case, I'd seen how the Manhattan DA's office treated detectives Bobby Addolorato and John Schwartz, then Steve Cohen, and even Dan Bibb, one of their own. And now they were looking into *me*?

The same week that the CIU lawyers interviewed JJ, Celia called me with what seemed like a monumental break involving Mustafa, the NYPD's "primary target" before JJ became a suspect.

Celia said a woman from Seattle had called saying that she'd been at a party where a friend named Mustafa, a drug dealer, started crying. She said he called up a website on her phone, freejonadrianvelazquez.com, which had been created by one of JJ's supporters. Mustafa scrolled to the sketch of the shooter, a black man with braids, and said: "That's me. There's a guy doing my time." And, she said, Mustafa had confessed to another friend as well. Bob and Celia spoke with both women and said they sounded credible.

Bob and Celia gave this information to Bonnie Sard, and a couple of weeks later the DA's office flew both women to New York for an interview. The first witness went into a conference room with the prosecutors. She came out looking shattered. "Why are they treating me like I'm a guilty person?" she said. "I was just trying to help. Why did we bother to come when no one wants to hear what we had to say?"

The Seattle women felt they were treated like suspects themselves—so much so that they asked Bob and Celia if they should get their own lawyer. Bob introduced them to Ron Kuby, a legendary New York defense attorney, who wrote a letter to the DA's office asking the CIU to deal with him in the future, because the women had just been trying to help and they felt like the DA's office was being hostile.

The day after he sent that letter, Kuby said the DA's office ignored his request and contacted the women directly. They had one question, and it wasn't about the case. It was: "Who told you to hire Ron Kuby?"

Kuby was furious. He called me to his office and suggested I film him writing the DA's office an email, so I did. Kuby wrote: "One of your detectives contacted my client after I asked them not to. Stop the misconduct . . . you're not above the law, so stop acting like it."

About a month after the DA's office interviewed the witnesses, I flew to Seattle and spoke with both women. They insisted that Mustafa had told them, independently, that he had been responsible for the shooting. And both women said they were treated disrespectfully by the Manhattan DA's CIU when they were flown to New York. One said: "The DA was more concerned about my personal life than Mustafa. For more than four hours they questioned me: Where do I work? Who am I dating? Do I have insurance? What if I get sick—how do I go to the hospital? Why am I not a citizen? Am I an alcoholic?"

While I was in Seattle, I showed up unannounced at Mustafa's house with a cameraperson and an armed bodyguard I'd hired. I knocked on a sliding glass door and Mustafa appeared.

"I wanted to talk to you about something that happened in New York," I said. "I'm from NBC News *Dateline*. I come to you in peace, man!"

Mustafa came out, smoking a cigarette. He was a Black man with short, braided hair and a long scar on his face.

I told him why I was there. He denied knowing anything about the crime. He not only said that he'd never committed a murder but also claimed he'd never told anyone that he did.

"I swear to God!" he kept saying. "I never shoot somebody! I never lived in Harlem!"

I wasn't sure what to think after we spoke. Mustafa was adamant he had no idea what I was talking about. He also had a strong accent, and none of the eyewitnesses had mentioned the shooter having one.

I called the women. Again they insisted that he had confessed to them.

Someone was lying. I just didn't know who.

The DA's office would later say they investigated Seattle Mustafa and ruled him out as a suspect. They said they found he had an alibi—he'd evidently been on a fishing boat in Alaska at the time of the murder.

But whether this Mustafa was involved with the crime or not, the real importance of that episode to me was how the witnesses said the DA's office treated them, seemingly trying to discredit them from the beginning.

In April 2013, seventeen months after the CIU began reinvestigating JJ's case, Sard delivered her decision in a sixteen-page letter to Bob and Celia.

Sard said they'd "taken seriously the claims you have raised" and that her office "had conducted an extensive reinvestigation which has included interviews of numerous witnesses and an in-depth review of documentary and physical evidence from a wide variety of sources." Their conclusion: "We cannot consent to your request to vacate Mr. Velazquez's conviction."

"In closing," Sard wrote, "we have conducted this reinvestigation with an open mind and committed the full force of our office's resources to this important task."

As I read the letter in disbelief and reviewed what Sard considered a "fair, objective and thorough" investigation, I noticed something that brazenly undercut that claim: the DA's office never even interviewed Maria and Vanessa, JJ's alibi witnesses.

Bob and Celia were equally enraged by the DA's decision, particularly because they'd wasted a year and a half waiting to file an appeal, at Sard's suggestion. In a press conference in front of the courthouse, Bob let loose, describing Vance's CIU as a "joke" and more of "a conviction protection racket." He said this even though he'd supported Vance's campaign and been on his transition team.

Speaking of Vance, JJ's mother, Maria, put it more simply: "We trusted him to bring us justice, and he didn't bring us justice."

Someone else was at that press conference: Dan Bibb, the former Manhattan assistant DA who had been ordered to defend the convictions of two innocent men in the Palladium case. Not only did Bibb believe JJ was innocent, but he also roundly criticized Vance's unit, saying it operated in bad faith with the same tunnel vision the office had employed in the Palladium case.

Vance's head of communications saw me at that press conference and got it into her head that I was somehow part of organizing it. She sent me an email saying, "It was weird to see you at the press conference coordinating. That was nasty."

I replied, copying others at the DA's office, saying that I had nothing to do with the press conference and didn't appreciate having my integrity questioned when I was covering a public event. She sent me back an email that read, simply: "Really? The entire office is cc'd? We're done communicating."

According to Barry Scheck, the goal of any CIU is to be open and collaborative, but Vance's CIU was adversarial and secretive. Instead of trying to get to the truth, it appeared more interested in protecting the office's convictions. A couple of years after it launched, I filed a Freedom of Information Act request asking for a list of everyone the unit had investigated and helped exonerate. I was told it wasn't public information. I later found out that the list had fewer than ten people on it.

After the CIU denied JJ's request to vacate his conviction, his attorneys spent hundreds of hours preparing an appeal to submit to the court, asking for a hearing. There seemed to be a lot of grounds for their argument. In that letter to JJ's attorneys denying JJ's request to vacate his conviction, Sard herself acknowledged that the DA's office had sent its own investigator to interview the key eyewitness, Augustus Brown, and the investigator signed an affidavit saying Brown told him that he picked JJ out at random. Another eyewitness, Phillip Jones, said he also knew JJ was the wrong man. But appeals take a long time. By the time Bob and Celia filed it, the DA's office replied, and Judge Abraham Clott made his decision about whether to hear it, nineteen more months would pass.

JJ heard the news at the end of 2014, a few weeks before Christmas. That night he wrote me a letter that sent a shiver of fear through me:

DECEMBER 5, 2014, 4:34 A.M.

Dear Dan:

It is with great regret that I must sit here at this lonely hour and inform you that "justice" has no place in my life. It seems as if "freedom" may not be on an immediate horizon for me and that "hope" is just a cruel joke! . . .

I'm writing this letter suffocating in this tiny ass cage, bruised and battered by a horrendous decision to overlook such a terrible travesty. I want to scream so loud, but it won't make sense because I'm not being heard. . . . Do I have to jump off a prison tier with a noose around my neck to get people to realize that wrongful convictions are a "slow death"? . . . Tell me, Dan, what is it going to take?

That letter was dated twelve years to the day that JJ had first written me, and almost twenty-four years to the day that Lemus and Hidalgo had been convicted in the Palladium case. When I read it at my desk, I wept openly. I didn't care who saw me.

I feared it would be the last letter JJ would ever write.

17 THE DAY JOB

I GET ASKED A lot why I "can't let anything go," why I'm so "relentless." It's not always framed as a compliment. I usually answer that all that matters is the truth. But I don't get paid by NBC for being obsessed by my outrage. I get paid to produce stories that actually make it to air.

My wrongful-conviction investigations were all mainly happening when I could fit them in, generally evenings and weekends. My day job during much of this time was being part of a robust investigative unit that specialized in producing daring hidden-camera reports unearthing scams and exploring hidden worlds. My boss was Allan Maraynes, a legendary producer who worked for many years at *60 Minutes* and was a pioneer in using hidden cameras to investigate wrongdoing. Allan encouraged me to think creatively and take risks.

I worked on a wide array of projects, from chasing Mexican drug cartels through the mountains of Utah with the DEA to investigating a bogus medical insurance company. I also conceived and produced several *Dateline* franchise series, perhaps the oddest of which was called *Wild, Wild Web*.

I'd been scrolling through Craigslist one day and came across some odd online ads, many offering unusual and often illegal activities. I pitched the idea that we answer those ads with hidden cameras and see what happened. The purpose was to shine a light on the dark underbelly of the digital world, but it was very strange work. I always had burner phones and fake email addresses. The people I met in the course of a day were not exactly people I wanted following me home. And I wound up in some very odd situations.

Working undercover, I encountered real hit men, purveyors of human body parts, and even self-styled vampires seeking to consume human blood. I went as a homeless person on the Vegas Strip to infiltrate a donations scam, and I met people looking to sell babies. The depths of human depravity that I witnessed often left me rattled. Sometimes our shows were just bizarre.

During one episode, former *Dateline* correspondent Chris Hansen and I met up with a scam artist named Jessica who posted suggestive photos of a woman she said was her (but who was really a former classmate) while asking an elderly man for thousands of dollars to be his girlfriend. Chris and I traveled to Texas, where Jessica lived, pretending to be the man's concerned nephews. We met her at a restaurant, wired with hidden cameras, and Chris confronted her about the lies she'd been telling and the fraud she tried to commit.

A couple of months after we aired the story, I was contacted by a viewer who found out Jessica had moved to Maine and started robbing houses she was hired to clean. So we rented a house in Maine, wired it with hidden cameras, and made an appointment with Jessica for a cleaning. Once we saw her start to steal from us on our hidden cameras, Chris walked downstairs and said, "Jessica! Again?"

Jessica took off running, a silly thing to do since we were in the middle of nowhere. Even sillier, we chased her; I have no idea why. I was running backward filming her jogging as Chris ran next to her, confronting her about her life of crime. I stumbled and wiped out, my back on the ground, my feet to the sky. Jessica looked over at me, clearly hoping I was injured, and kept jogging. When I speak at journalism schools, I'm always tempted to show students that clip, which fortunately never aired, to illustrate just how bonkers a day can be when you do this sort of work.

It felt great when our reporting made an impact, like the investigation I did on "bath salts," a synthetic drug that was being sold over the counter at gas stations and head shops. People were snorting it, and many were dying as a result. It was so new that the FDA had not yet regulated it. Wearing a hidden camera, I went to the East Village to show how easy it was to buy. Then I wondered, who were the big suppliers? So I went undercover as a businessman looking to invest in someone selling the drug. I simply went to Google and typed "Where can I buy bath salts in bulk?" I had plenty of choices.

I ended up meeting with a man from Minneapolis who told me he made his own mixture of the substance. "I'm a fucking mad chemist, dude," he said as I recorded him in his warehouse on a hidden camera. He said he'd made a quarter of a million dollars in four months. When I asked him if he used the stuff himself, he acted like I was insane.

A few days before we aired the bath salts story, I called my old friend lawyer Steve Cohen from the Palladium case, who was now Governor Andrew Cuomo's top deputy. Steve had a lot of power in New York, and the same week my show aired, the New York State Department of Health classified the drug as illegal.

I felt there was integrity to the kind of work I was doing on *Dateline*. There was certainly entertainment value. And yet it wasn't what interested me most. After I got home at the end of a day chasing scammers or going undercover, I'd catch up with Jocelyn, play with Casey, and then stay up half the night reading police reports, trial transcripts, and court briefs.

My obsession was how obviously broken our justice system was. While my work on false imprisonment was a big part of that, it wasn't the only part. My innocence work had become a way into understanding the tragic consequences of America's system of mass incarceration—for the innocent, the guilty, and all of society. I felt a need to do these stories as often as I could convince my bosses to give me the airtime. And I couldn't have asked for a better partner than Lester Holt, a remarkable human being and friend.

According to a 2018 survey published by the *Hollywood Reporter*, Lester is the most trusted news personality in America; his professionalism is only buoyed by his kindness. When Lester is fronting a report, you know it's worthy and important. Over the years, we covered many stories together calling attention to the ways justice is denied, whether by wrongful convictions or because of the humanitarian disaster that is Rikers Island.

Among the highest-profile stories Lester and I did was about the rapper Meek Mill. Jay-Z had written an op-ed about his friend Meek, explaining how impossible it could be for a Black man to escape from years of probation and monitoring even if the original crime was nonviolent and committed when he was young. Meek had been arrested on gun and drug possession charges as a teenager. He served eight months but was on probation for more than a decade. A Philadelphia judge threw him back in prison at the age of thirty for violating that probation by popping a wheelie on a motorcycle.

Desiree Perez, the CEO of Jay-Z's Roc Nation, teamed up with Meek's friend Michael Rubin, a billionaire co-owner of the Philadelphia 76ers, to publicize the outrage of Meek's story. Soon #FreeMeek had become a social media sensation and a movement for millions demanding reform.

My senior producer, Paul Ryan, suggested I go to Philadelphia to start shooting interviews about Meek's case. As I was sitting across from Rubin at his desk, cameras running, Rubin got a call from the governor's office informing him that Meek was getting clemency and would be released that evening.

Rubin decided to pick him up from prison in a helicopter and take him straight to a basketball game. He said Meek once told him he'd had a dream that would happen. The 76ers were playing the Boston Celtics in the Eastern Conference Finals. Within minutes I was in a helicopter taping as Meek was airlifted out of prison and straight to the game.

That moment was not just about the release of a rapper; it was about a community coming together to support one of its own. The moment Meek walked out of that prison it seemed to transcend sports and music—not just for Meek but also for countless people for whom his plight had become a rallying cry. As Meek rang the opening bell at the game that evening, the cheers of the crowd were deafening.

To both Lester and me, shining a light on mass incarceration is a moral obligation. In 2019, we decided to tackle the topic in a way that had never before been done. We conceived a weeklong series called *Justice for All*, for which every show on NBC News and MSNBC would do stories about criminal justice reform. As part of the series, I proposed that MSNBC host a town hall from Sing Sing, the first town hall ever to be held at a maximum-security prison. And for a *Dateline* hour, we would lock up Lester (and me along with him) for a couple of nights at the Louisiana State Penitentiary, known as Angola. Putting someone America loved in a prison cell and filming it would help people understand the prison system in a way nothing else would.

The experience was full of surprises. Seth Smith, the second-in-charge of Louisiana corrections, is a tough, strong guy. And he said, "What we're doing is just not working."

"That's *you* saying this?" I said.

"Yeah, we just can't lock them up and throw away the key. We got to give people hope!"

After we were granted access to Angola, I interviewed more than a hundred prisoners over the course of several months. It's a producer's job to manage all the advance work—the interviews, the logistics, the angles. If you're good at your job, much of your work is an invisible ballet that makes things go smoothly on the day of taping, so that when the on-air talent shows up, they can step into the frame and do what they do best—telling the story.

I'd logged countless hours in Angola by the time Lester arrived, and then there we were: Lester and me in side-by-side cells in the maximum-security prison. It was loud. It was bright. It was incredibly uncomfortable.

We didn't have the full prison experience, of course. I had my cellphone in case of an emergency, and we knew we'd get out the next day. It was just a really bad hotel room. But the whole crew was impressed when Lester fell asleep minutes after his cell door closed. Noise or light meant nothing to him. *That's a man with a clear conscience*, I thought, watching him doze in the middle of hell.

In our conversations with people spending twenty-three hours a day in a cement box, Lester and I kept looking at each other as if to say, *Really? Beyond redemption? All of them?*

If the answer is no, are we *creating* people to be beyond redemption?

I spent forty-five minutes in the prison's hospice ward talking to a guy who was frail and bedridden. *Is he a danger?* I thought. *Does he need to be in here? Shouldn't we let him die with his family?*

Another man we met was Dalton Prejean Jr. He was ten years old when his father was executed at Angola for killing a state trooper at age seventeen. Now the younger Prejean was there himself serving a sixty-year sentence for shaking a one-year-old baby to death when the child wouldn't stop crying. Inside, he's become an inspirational leader to his fellow prisoners. He writes sermons and poems.

We asked to see the oldest man at Angola, and were introduced to Sammy Robinson, a man in his eighties who'd been locked up more than sixty years for a crime he committed as a teenager. Two years after I met him, he passed away.

What Lester and I hoped to do with these stories was shine a light on mass incarceration and wrongful convictions. Back in New York, JJ was helping us do that. From inside Sing Sing, he was turning into a one-man Innocence Project.

"I think you might want to speak with Johnny Hincapie," he told me one day.

"Jesus," I said. "There's *another* one in there?"

18   THE TOURIST SUBWAY MURDER

THERE WAS A TIME when I believed the old adage "Everyone in prison says they're innocent." Not anymore. Sure, some might say, "I was overcharged. I should be done already," or minimize their involvement, and yes, sometimes people out-and-out lie. But in my experience the overwhelming majority of people in prison admit that they committed the crime for which they were convicted. And when I've looked into the cases of people who said they were wrongly convicted, I've been shocked to learn that an alarming number were telling the truth.

Johnny Hincapie, who lived in Sing Sing's honor block with JJ, insisted he was one of those people. His case took me back again to 1990, the terrible year in New York of the Central Park Five trial, the Palladium murder, and the random stabbing of Brian Watkins, the crime for which Johnny was convicted.

When I first met Johnny, he'd already been locked up for more than two decades. He was a slender, even-tempered Colombian American from Queens who'd grown up wanting to be a nightclub dancer. Eager to tell me about the time before he came to prison, he shared stories of his life as a Bayside teenager almost like he was recounting a fairy tale set in some magical land.

In the 1980s, Johnny got his start in New York nightlife handing out flyers for a local nightclub called Avanti, and vowed that he'd become a singer, dancer, or DJ. By the time he was eighteen he'd done promotion for a bunch of clubs of that era—places with names like Lamour's East, Heartthrobs, and The Sound Factory. He got some gigs dancing, including—he said this with evident pride—in a few music videos.

His last day of freedom came on Labor Day weekend 1990, in the midst of the crime-ridden era that tore the city apart. The brutal rape of a jogger in Central Park was still fresh on the minds of New Yorkers, the C&C gang owned the Bronx, and the Palladium murder was two months away from happening. When Brian Watkins was stabbed on a Midtown subway platform, the city's pressure cooker exploded.

Watkins, a twenty-two-year-old college student and tennis player, was visiting New York with his family to attend the US Open. But the matches were delayed that night, so the Watkins family ended up out later than they'd anticipated and left the Sheraton Hotel in Manhattan around nine thirty with a plan to eat dinner in Greenwich Village. Instead of taking a cab, they made the fateful decision to take the subway. As they waited for their train on the platform at 53rd Street and Seventh Avenue, another train arrived from Queens with dozens of teenagers headed to the Roseland Ballroom for a night of dancing.

The train doors opened and a crowd spilled out, heading upstairs toward Roseland. But about a half dozen kids stayed behind. They didn't have enough money for the cover charge, so they decided they'd mug someone to get it, and the Watkins family was the group's random target.

One of the teenagers allegedly shouted, "It's killing time!" and someone cut Brian Watkins's father's pants pocket with a box cutter, slashing him in the process, to get to his wallet. His mother was grabbed, pulled down, and kicked in the face. Then a teenager named Gary Morales pulled out a knife and stabbed Brian. He and his friends took off with about $200 as a fresh-faced kid, who was in New York because he loved tennis, bled to death and his mother screamed for help. It was the city's 1,585th homicide of 1990.

A team of Manhattan detectives, including one who'd been involved with the arrest of the Central Park Five, began rounding up teenagers and questioning them. By the next day, cops said seven suspects had confessed on videotape. They were arrested and paraded in front of cameras. Their photos were all over the news with headlines like "WOLF PACK."

One of them was Johnny Hincapie, the only one of those convicted who said later he was coerced by police into making a false confession. He swore that he wasn't on the subway platform at all during the robbery.

This is what Johnny said happened: Headed for a night of dancing at the Roseland Ballroom, he took the Q13 bus from Bayside to Flushing. There, he ran into some friends who were also headed to the Roseland, and together they hopped on the 7 train to go into the city. His designer pants didn't have pockets, so he asked a friend, Anthony, to hold his wallet. They transferred to the E and at some point he lost sight of Anthony.

Once they got to the Midtown Manhattan station near Roseland, he said he started looking around for his friend. He kept asking people if they'd seen him but suddenly heard screaming and joined a flood of people running out of the station. Johnny didn't think too much about it; this was, after all, New York in the nineties. He danced the night away at Roseland and got a ride home late that night from a friend he knew as "Lemon."

The next day, as he was hanging out with his girlfriend at home, his mother asked him to come to the door. The police were there with some questions.

Johnny was eager to please people in authority, and he respected and trusted the police. And so, he told me, he was completely unprepared for what happened when he was taken from his home, assured by the officers that he didn't need a lawyer, and brought to the Midtown North police precinct.

He was taken into a room, he said, with bunk beds, on one of which a tough-seeming character was reclining and smoking a cigarette. Two other detectives asked if Johnny was hungry or thirsty. He said yes and they left him alone with a cop they identified simply as Detective Casey.

"He's blowing smoke into my face from the cigarette that he's smoking," Johnny recalled. "He slapped me in my face, pulled my hair, walked in front of me, and placed his foot on my chest and pushed me down to the floor while I was still handcuffed to the chair."

The more Johnny said he knew nothing about the robbery, the more Casey told him he was lying. He said that if Johnny wanted to go home, he should admit he was involved.

"Why are you being so mean?" Johnny said he asked the detective, sobbing.

"He said that for lying I was going to be put away for a very long time," Johnny told me. "I can't remember how many times I said to him that I was not lying, but I said it to him again and again, even though I was being told to 'shut up' by him.

"After a long silent pause, Detective Casey said that if I wanted to go home that night, all I had to do was memorize a story, that it was to my benefit, that if I did, he would have me driven back home immediately. I asked, 'If my attorney was here, what would he say about me memorizing a story?' He then said my attorney would tell me to do likewise."

Something people should know: Cops can lie. It's legal, and it's often used as a tactic to get people to confess. Just recently, nine states enacted reforms banning deceiving *children*—juveniles in custodial interrogations. New York isn't one of them. That's as far as we've come.[1]

Hincapie said he memorized the story, which was that he had witnessed the robbery and played a minor part in it. Once he was able to repeat the account, the other detectives came in with a burger and soda and uncuffed him so he could eat.

He was then made to repeat the story for an assistant district attorney while Casey made "intimidating eye contact" with him. When he was done, Johnny said, "Detective Casey gave me a thumbs up, which convinced me I was going to be able to go home. Moments later, someone came for me, took me outside the room, and started to fingerprint me. As tears started coming down my face, I realized in that moment that Detective Casey had lied to me, and I was not going home after all."

Johnny and six other teenagers from his neighborhood were arrested for the murder of Brian Watkins. But when I interviewed him more than two decades after the crime, Johnny insisted he hadn't been on the platform that night. As a middle-aged man at Sing Sing, he implored me to believe him.

Johnny seemed like a sincere, clean-cut guy. His mother, Maria, and father, Carlos, were religious and proud of Johnny and his brother, Alex. Johnny had never been in trouble before. He had never once been arrested until that night.

But who knew if he was telling the truth? Given the high-profile nature of the crime and the seven defendants who all allegedly confessed on videotape, I knew it would take forever just to collect all the information, like the videos and the paperwork—again, thousands of pages—and sort out the facts, especially because I was busy working on other stories. But eventually I made time to dig into the videos and stack of documents and learned more about what had happened that night.

People I tell about Johnny Hincapie often insist that they can't imagine confessing to something they didn't do, that they'd stay strong no matter what the cops said or how long they were locked up or how much violence they were subjected to, but studies have shown something different.[2] It's a fact: most of us are not as strong as we think we are. The average time people who falsely confessed were interrogated? Sixteen hours.[3] You're hungry. You're scared. You're tired. You just want to go home. And it happens a lot more than you'd think. False confessions have been shown to be involved in 29 percent of DNA exonerations.[4]

Johnny made it through only three hours of interrogation before he gave his statement. When I first watched the confession tapes of Johnny and the six others he was arrested with, I was struck by how very young they all were. Johnny was a skinny kid with a ponytail. Not surprisingly, kids and teens are particularly vulnerable to falsely confessing. The human brain doesn't fully develop until age twenty-five, which limits the ability to fully understand long-term consequences.[5]

There are ways to reduce the possibility of a false confession, beginning with recording all interrogations so that it's clear what treatment and what representation of facts led up to the suspect's statement. I wonder if Johnny Hincapie's confession would have stood up in court if such a recording had been done in his case.

And yet, after that confession, he was convicted and spent sixteen years in prison before anyone started looking into his case. That happened when a reporter named Bill Hughes interviewed two others convicted in the Watkins case—Gary Morales, who had stabbed Brian Watkins, and Emiliano Fernandez, who had slashed Watkins's father with the box cutter. Both told Hughes that Johnny wasn't on the platform that night, and Hughes also watched original interrogation footage in which a third suspect also said Johnny hadn't been there. Hughes published a story about Johnny's plight in a nonprofit paper called *City Limits* but, he later said, "nobody really cared."[6]

Johnny kept trying to tell people what had happened to him. A couple of years later, in one of the college courses he took at Sing Sing, he met a former chairman of the New York State Parole Board named Bob Dennison, who after hearing Johnny's story, teamed up with Hughes to do a full reinvestigation of the case. They called themselves the Irish Guys Gumshoe Squad, and after another year of looking they found a new witness: Luis Montero, who had been at the subway station that night. Montero confirmed what Johnny said—that he was upstairs, looking for his friend Anthony.

Montero hadn't come forward before, he said, because he was scared. As it turns out, he'd also been accused of the same crime all those years ago and done eighteen months in Rikers awaiting trial before prosecutors realized they had the wrong guy. He said he'd been beaten during his interrogation too, but he hadn't cracked like Johnny had.

Still, Johnny remained in prison until Ron Kuby, who also had a role in JJ's case, offered to represent him pro bono. In light of Montero's coming forward, Kuby eventually persuaded Judge Eduardo Padro to give Johnny a hearing.

As the hearing approached, I petitioned Judge Padro for permission to film in the courtroom. He granted my request, and in the fall of 2015 I saw Johnny sitting anxiously at the defense table and his parents, Maria and Carlos, and his brother, Alex, sitting behind him in the courtroom crying. His mother never let go of the rosary beads in her hands.

The Watkins killing was the last straw for the residents of New York City. It had been just a year since a jogger had been raped in Central Park. Fear ruled the streets. There were daily news stories with people saying things like "I dress for the muggers."[7] By now, it wasn't a stretch for me to believe that if the NYPD and the Manhattan DA had gotten the jogger case wrong, they could be wrong about this one too.

The Brian Watkins case raised questions about that era of strict sentencing. Why were seven teenagers put away for the rest of their lives when most of them were just standing by when the stabbing took place? Does that make society safer? Does that provide solace for the victim's family?

I was eager to hear what kind of evidence the Manhattan DA's office would present to keep Johnny in prison. The ADA assigned to defend the conviction was Eugene Hurley, the same prosecutor who had taken JJ to trial fifteen years earlier.

Luis Montero testified and confirmed Johnny's story. Johnny took the stand too, and Kuby asked him whether he had testified in his original trial. He said no—his original lawyer had told him not to.

"I wanted to take the stand," Johnny said. "He told me that the district attorney's office would basically just walk all over me, because I had confessed."

Johnny told the court his version of events and described how aggressive the officer interrogating him had been until he confessed: "He slapped my face. He grabbed me by my hair." He also shared jailhouse letters, including one from two days after he was arrested, begging someone to explain to the judge that he was telling the truth about the detective instructing him on what to say.

"I was just eighteen years old when this happened," Johnny said when he was asked for a final statement, "and I never had a chance. I never had an opportunity, your honor, from the moment that I was arrested. Not one chance."

Then it came time for Hurley's cross-examination.

"And it is the first time that you have ever alleged to a court that your confession was coerced by Detective Casey physically abusing you and making you memorize a story," said Hurley. "Is that correct?"

"Correct," said Hincapie.

Hurley said the jailhouse letters could have been forged, the dates changed. As for the letter in question, Hurley said it was "conveniently addressed to an attorney who is now dead." Hurley then accused Johnny of lying. "In fact, you waited for him to pass away to forge that letter to him, didn't you?"

"Not at all, sir," said Hincapie.

Then Hurley mocked Johnny's story of a cop abusing him.

"He was wearing a T-shirt, smoking cigarettes, right? Like some evil movie cop?"

"Yes," Hincapie said.

"You made that up, didn't you?"

"No," Hincapie said, reduced to tears as he had been in the interrogation room. "It was not true, Mr. Hurley."

But Johnny's defense attorney Ron Kuby wasn't done. In the middle of the hearing, a surprise witness named Mariluz Santana surfaced. She had read about the hearing and came forward to say that she'd been on the platform that night and ran off when she saw the teens heading for the Watkins family. On the stand, she testified that she saw the attackers and that Johnny, whom she knew from their neighborhood, wasn't one of them.

Judge Padro announced his decision a few months later, on October 6, 2015.

He said there was not enough evidence to definitively declare Johnny actually innocent. But he wrote that the testimony of the new witnesses would have changed the outcome of the first trial.

"All three witnesses indicate that Hincapie was not on the subway platform at the actual moment of the robbery of the Watkins family," Padro wrote. "Each statement exculpates Mr. Hincapie."

With that reasoning, Padro declared from the bench that he was setting aside Johnny's conviction. Hincapie burst into tears, as did his parents and brother. Applause erupted inside the courtroom.

But then, seconds later, prosecutor Eugene Hurley asked the judge to keep Johnny in prison while the DA's office decided whether to retry him.

Ron Kuby had an angry response. "Let's not ignore that Mr. Hincapie has been incarcerated for twenty-five years, one month, and, as of today, three days," Kuby said. "He's made a quarter-century liberty down payment."

Padro agreed and released Johnny on $1 bail. Processing him out took six hours. Then Johnny, his face wet with tears, walked out to a large group of family and friends and a gaggle of reporters before heading to his first dinner since he was eighteen that wasn't behind bars.

In acting unusually decisively and quickly, Judge Padro seemed like a judicial outlier, and Johnny Hincapie couldn't believe his luck. But his ruling was also a remarkable lesson in how random and subjective decisions on false imprisonment can be. To me, there was a mountain more evidence pointing to the innocence of other men I'd investigated, like JJ, who were still in prison. And even though Johnny was free, he still had to live with the fear that prosecutors would come after him again during the two years it took the Manhattan DA's office to make its decision, the same time it took in David Lemus's case.

In the end, the DA said that while his office still thought Johnny was guilty, he had already served twenty-five years and the memories of witnesses wouldn't be as reliable anymore, so they were dropping the case.

Johnny was a terrified kid who'd never been in trouble and went to church every Sunday. He believed it when the police said he could go home if he just said he was at the scene of the Watkins murder. Instead, he was locked up for twenty-five years—and no one in the NYPD faced consequences for that.

I was with Johnny and his family hours after he was released, and so was Lester Holt, who had been working with me on Johnny's story. When our *Dateline* hour about Johnny appeared in October 2015, reported by Lester, Johnny Hincapie was a free man. But JJ was still in Sing Sing.

19   11/11

ON NOVEMBER 11, 2015, JJ turned forty. He'd been locked up for eighteen years and he was no closer to freedom.

His mother always went to Sing Sing to see him on his birthday, but she never looked forward to it. As the years passed, Maria, like her grandchildren, found it harder to make herself visit him in prison. "I don't like seeing him there," she said. "He's gotten old. Every time I see him it hurts. When I think about the fact that he's lost all those years, that he's never going to get that back—I try not to think about it, but it does come into my mind. Especially on his birthday."

By now I'd known JJ a long time. When I met him, my daughter, Casey, wasn't even born; now she had turned twelve. Each one of Casey's milestones—moving from a crib to a big-kid bed, starting school, entering middle school—was a reminder of JJ's unending imprisonment.

In September 2016, the appellate court ruled on JJ's request for a hearing. The verdict from a three-judge panel was unanimous: request denied. Although they never heard any testimony, the judges found the recantations of the two eyewitnesses "highly suspect."

They also weighed in on the Seattle Mustafa story, which, the court said, "was refuted by the overwhelming evidence the people unearthed in their re-investigation of the crime."

Bob and Celia were devastated by the decision. I was outraged. As far as the DA's office was concerned, JJ was done. Unless new evidence surfaced, that was the end of the line, legally speaking.

Ever since I'd started as an intern at NBC, I'd worked hard to be an objective, thorough reporter concerned only with the facts. In all of my investigations, I'm mindful of maintaining a rigorous detachment. And from the beginning, my mantra to JJ, as to everyone who tells me they are innocent, was that if I found anything that proved his guilt, I would report it, because I'm an advocate for the truth, not for him.

JJ had heard me say that a thousand times. This boundary was as much for JJ's protection as for mine. The district attorney's office made my reporting an issue, and I was mindful that all my conversations with JJ from Sing Sing were recorded and monitored. And I had a responsibility to NBC and to journalistic ethics. So like always, I made sure he was clear that I am a reporter and will follow the story wherever it goes.

But the truth was I'd gotten to the point in my reporting where I was sure JJ was innocent and couldn't pretend there were two sides to his story anymore. There was only one reality. And as a father, as a human being, I couldn't help but be moved by what JJ's wrongful imprisonment had cost him and his family.

Still, I kept repeating my mantra.

After JJ's latest appeal had been denied, I was standing in the lobby of the courthouse at 111 Centre Street, shaken, when JJ called me from Sing Sing for an update. I heard the hope in his voice.

I delivered the bad news and then—because I saw a prosecutor from the Manhattan DA's office within earshot and I wanted to put my objectivity on display—I made sure to repeat my mantra yet again.

There was a long pause. Then I heard JJ say, his voice cracking, "Really, Dan? Now?"

I can hardly even think about that moment.

I'd known JJ fourteen years by then, I'd visited him more than 150 times, and I was pretty sure there was nothing else to uncover, nothing else to find. JJ was innocent as surely as he was alive.

Not only was JJ clearly innocent, but he was an exceptional person as well. I'd seen his integrity in the forbearance and forgiveness he manifested even though his life had been stolen from him.

While I have a responsibility to the truth, I also have a responsibility to be a decent person, and it has been a tricky thing to navigate in my dealings with false imprisonment and the men who had suffered because of it. And that moment in the courthouse was one time when I was not living up to my obligations as a human being. I was behaving in a way I was taught to behave.

That rigidity, that lack of humanity, that desire to appear ethical, is why people are wrongfully convicted in the first place.

I never again said those words to JJ. It was a turning point in our relationship, at least for me.

My conversations with JJ started to become as much about him as about his case. He would tell me horrible stories of what life was like on the inside. How dehumanizing it all was. How so many of the rules made no sense. "Do you know I could get written up for giving food to a friend who is hungry?" he told me.

He explained how freezing it was during the winter months, and how even with layers of clothes and a blanket, he would be up all night shivering. Every cell has a tiny sink with one button that dispenses only cold water, flowing through pipes more than a century old. He described what it felt like to be locked down for a week or two at a time when the prison faced a security issue. Twenty-four hours a day inside a locked cell. No hot water. No phone or communication. No showers. It would be enough to break the strongest among us.

But if anything, the years of suffering seemed to be focusing JJ like a prize-fighter in training. He began to work harder, both for himself and for others. He immersed himself in programs and began to take college courses offered by a nonprofit called Hudson Link for Higher Education, ultimately graduating with a bachelor's degree in behavioral science. At the commencement ceremony held in the prison's visiting room, I watched as JJ and his fellow graduates wore caps and gowns over their green prison pants. The commencement speaker was Whoopi Goldberg. Harry Belafonte was there too.

After JJ graduated, he began working for Hudson Link on the inside. Even as he struggled to make it through another day, week, month, year, he was always working to give hope to others, mainly encouraging other incarcerated men to enroll in school. I've lost count of how many men inside Sing Sing have told me, "If it wasn't for JJ . . ."

He became so respected on the inside that he was elected by Sing Sing's incarcerated population to represent them to the prison administration when any issues arose.

"He was a natural leader," Michael Capra, the superintendent (or warden) of Sing Sing, once told me. "Here's a guy who reminds you of a CEO from the beginning. There's an air about him. He's very clear. He reads the room very well. He stepped up as a young professional, like an executive in a company."

When you think of a tough guy, you picture Superintendent Capra, who'd worked for the New York State Department of Corrections for four decades, starting out as a corrections officer and working his way up to the top job at Sing Sing in 2012, around the same time my *Dateline* hour about JJ aired. He'd seen the show I'd done and he'd noticed how JJ was organizing other incarcerated men, who admitted their guilt, to help them redefine what it meant to pay a debt to society.

People who work in corrections aren't in a position to comment about whether someone should be in prison or not. And yet, within the limits of his position, Capra worked hard to create opportunities for JJ as well as the fifteen hundred other men at Sing Sing. He wanted to help them find new ways to discourage kids from making the same mistakes they had. So in 2013 he called and asked to meet with me to discuss my interest in helping a small group of incarcerated men make a video about gun violence.

I loved the sound of the project, but even more important to me was keeping JJ's spirits up. I began to volunteer, and together with the help of my NBC colleagues and friends Rob Allen, Rich White, and Rick Albright, we made a video called *Voices from Within*.

The way we did it was this: We went into the prison and set up a camera pointing at a chair. One by one, incarcerated men went into the room alone and talked into the lens. They were talking to the kids in their old neighborhood, but you got the feeling that really they were talking to their younger selves. You could see it on their faces and hear it in their voices that they had true remorse and wanted more than anything to make amends in whatever way they could. They took responsibility. They held themselves accountable. They embraced their shame. And almost all were overcome with emotion and broke down.

Among the statements the men made to the camera:

"I shot my friend six times because I was angry."

"I know how it feels to have eliminated a name, to have destroyed a family. You can't make it right."

And: "They're trying to build a life and then something bad happens to them. I'm the bad thing that happens to them. You could be the bad thing that happens to someone."

He went on to say that if you participated in gun violence, then that cell, that prison yard, could become your "new now."

The video let at-risk kids see for themselves what it looks and feels like if you're put in prison. This was not *Scared Straight*—prisoners yelling at kids, trying to terrify them. Those programs were shown to be unsuccessful because, it turned out, kids admired the toughness of the incarcerated men and wanted to be like them.[1] In these videos, the men look into the eyes of the kids and tell them just how bad it is to be where they are. They talk about how much they're missing now, how sad they are, how sad their mothers and children are. Quietly and steadily, they tell the truth.

Superintendent Capra helped spread the message of taking responsibility and being vulnerable around the prison. Describing the men working on *Voices from Within*, he said, "They want to give back to their own peer group, you guys. The point of it is: everybody can be successful."

Over the years, I came to consider Superintendent Capra a close friend, and a profoundly credible messenger inside the system who doesn't paint everyone with the same brush. He's far from soft. He will tear your head off if needed, but he notices the nuanced differences in each person's humanity and potential. He calls himself "a student of human behavior."

While Capra knew he had no power to shorten or lengthen anyone's sentence, he made it his mission for as many men as possible to leave his prison with more education and integrity than they had when they came in. It was his purpose. When a new group of incarcerated men arrived at Sing Sing, Capra would give them what he called his "Father Mike" speech: "I know one thing for sure. None of you were born to come to prison."

Over time, I saw Superintendent Capra's relationship evolve with the men who created *Voices from Within*. What started as a video turned into a program that greatly helped the men who cofounded it. One by one they were released and went on to do incredible things on the outside. Lawrence Bartley works for the Marshall Project, a nonprofit news organization that focuses on criminal justice issues, and he fronted a series for Vice TV called *Inside Story*. Laron Rogers is employed by the Fortune Society, a nonprofit that helps people reenter society after incarceration. Colin Absolam works for the Osbourne Association, whose mission is to strengthen the families of those affected by incarceration. Dario Peña works for the Center for Justice at Columbia University. Sean Kyler works for the Vera Institute for Justice. Jermaine Archer works in philanthropy. Markey Coleman got his real estate license. Andre Jenkins runs his own company.

Kenyatta Hughes, the one who talked about the "new now," sang at Carnegie Hall eight hours after his release, thanks to a program called Musical Connections that Carnegie runs at Sing Sing. He'd served twenty-two years for murder. The concert was called his "first free note," and every song he sang he'd written in prison.

I was there that night. It was unbelievable. With complete confidence and a gorgeous voice, he sang: "How many guns does one man need? How many children have to bleed?" and "The way things are is not the way they have to be." People throughout the hall, including me, were weeping. At the end of the concert, Kenyatta led a singalong with the audience, who gave him a standing ovation.

There was someone else sitting in the front row with me at that concert: JJ's mom, Maria. She'd come out to support Kenyatta, but her son was still locked away, and I was more determined than ever not to leave his side. If I'd been in JJ's place, I would have lost my mind. But he'd become a leader. He could have become cynical or angry. Instead, he took his feeling of despair and turned it into fuel to help other people in prison with him.

JJ provided me with an immersive education about the humanity concealed behind prison walls, regardless of someone's innocence or guilt, and how much more humane the system should be. And he also taught me something else: how easy it is to find an innocent person behind bars.

I'd thought I'd heard it all. That's when JJ told me about the truly disturbing case of Richard Rosario.

Pall over Palladium
Club bouncer shot to death

By DAVID BURCH
Special to The News

BOUNCER SLAIN: Marcus Peterson, 23, was killed after refusing to readmit two men to the Palladium.

On Thanksgiving night in 1990, a bouncer was murdered at the Palladium nightclub in Manhattan, the latest in a string of highly publicized crimes in the city that received sensational coverage, like this story in the New York *Daily News*. Two innocent men would be found guilty of the crime. (NY *Daily News*)

Mug shots of David Lemus (*top left*) and Olmedo Hidalgo (*top right*), who were wrongly convicted of committing the Palladium murder, and of Thomas "Spanky" Morales (*bottom left*) and Joey Pillot, who were the real culprits. (New York Police Department)

NYPD detectives John Schwartz and Bobby Addolorato of the Bronx Homicide Task Force work at Bronx detective headquarters, also known as Fort Apache, 2002. Both detectives eventually retired in frustration after prosecutors rebuffed their attempts to prove that the wrong men had been convicted of the Palladium murder. (NBC News)

David Lemus and Olmedo Hidalgo describe their ordeal in an interview with *Dateline*, 2002. (NBC News)

LEFT: Dan Slepian visits with David Lemus at Green Haven Correctional Facility in August 2002, three years before Lemus was released. (Dan Slepian)

BELOW: Although Manhattan assistant district attorney Dan Bibb reinvestigated the Palladium shootings and concluded that Lemus and Hidalgo had been wrongly convicted, he says he was ordered to defend their convictions. (NBC News)

David Lemus on the day of his release, October 19, 2005, after serving fifteen years in prison. (NBC News)

A-Block in Sing Sing Correctional Facility, one of the largest prison housing units in the country and where Jon-Adrian "JJ" Velazquez was initially imprisoned before being moved to what's known in the prison as "honors block," and officially as "preferred housing." (Dan Slepian)

Dan Slepian's first taped interview with JJ, in 2007, nearly five years after they met. (NBC News)

JJ's sons: Jacob, ten, and Jon Jr., thirteen, 2008. (Dan Slepian)

Eric Glisson, shown in his cell in Sing Sing in 2012, had just become a new father when he was arrested for murdering a cabdriver in the Bronx. He was one of what the media called the "Bronx Six," who were all wrongly convicted of the murder despite the lack of any forensic or physical evidence linking them to the crime. JJ told Dan Slepian about Glisson's case. (Dan Slepian)

ABOVE: A 1995 *New York* magazine story celebrated NYPD detectives Mike Donnelly and Thomas Aiello, who claimed to have solved two murders falsely attributed to the Bronx Six—the cabdriver and a thirty-eight-year-old woman. All seven people they arrested for the murders were innocent, and six were wrongly convicted (*New York*)

RIGHT: Eric Glisson's first minutes of freedom after nearly eighteen years in prison, 2012. (NBC News)

TOP: The *New York Post* front page several days after the stabbing death of Brian Watkins, a tourist from Utah, in a New York subway station in 1990. The murder forever changed policing in New York City. (*New York Post*)

MIDDLE: Johnny Hincapie, one of seven teenagers charged in the Watkins murder and sentenced to twenty-five years to life, 2015. (NBC News)

BOTTOM: Richard Rosario at Sullivan County Correctional Facility, 2014. He was convicted of a murder in the Bronx despite providing detectives with the names of thirteen alibi witnesses who confirmed he was in Florida at the time of the killing. (NBC News)

ABOVE: JJ spent hundreds of hours working in his cell at Sing Sing, often late into the night, learning the law and writing letters on behalf of himself and others. (NBC News)

LEFT: Dan Slepian with *NBC Nightly News* and *Dateline* anchor Lester Holt, filming in Times Square, 2015. (Dan Slepian)

BELOW: JJ and Dan Slepian in Sing Sing's honor block yard, fifteen years after they first met, 2017. (Sean Gallagher)

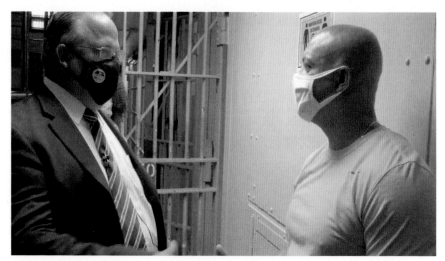

Sing Sing superintendent Michael Capra tells JJ that New York governor Andrew Cuomo has granted him clemency and he is going to be released, 2021. (NBC News)

JJ is embraced by his mother, Maria, and his two sons after his release from Sing Sing, 2021. He served twenty-three years, seven months, and eight days in prison. (NBC News)

One year after his release, JJ delivers a speech in Denver, "The Never-Ending Impact of Incarceration," in his role as a program director for the Frederick Douglass Project for Justice. (Stand Together Foundation)

DESPITE ALL I'D ALREADY learned about wrongful convictions, when JJ first told me about Richard Rosario's case, I literally couldn't believe it. I was surprised that I could still be surprised.

Richard's claim was nothing short of astonishing. He said he had been convicted and sentenced to twenty-five years to life for a murder in the Bronx despite giving police the names of not one or two but *thirteen* witnesses who could swear he was a thousand miles away in Florida at the time of the crime for which he was convicted. The number left me dumbfounded. How could I not investigate this one?

It didn't take long to learn the basic details of his case. At one thirty in the afternoon on June 19, 1996, a seventeen-year-old named Jorge Collazo and his friend Michael Sanchez were walking together near the corner of White Plains Road and Turnbull Avenue in the South Bronx. In the middle of a big parking lot, two other men walked toward them. They bumped shoulders and exchanged some heated words. According to police reports, it was a "random encounter."

Jorge Collazo and Michael Sanchez kept walking down the street. The other two men split up. One followed Collazo and Sanchez; the other headed to a getaway car waiting on the corner. The one who followed Collazo and Sanchez walked up behind them and shot Jorge point-blank in the face but didn't touch Sanchez. The shooter ran to the getaway car, and he and his buddy were gone as quickly as it all happened.

The general details seemed to fly in the face of any notion that it was a "random encounter." Why would a bump in a parking lot cause an execution? Why was only Jorge shot? Why was there a getaway car? Already something didn't add up.

Police arrived and found two eyewitnesses: Michael Sanchez, the victim's friend, and Robert Davis, a custodian in a building a couple of car lengths away from where the shooting happened. Both Sanchez and Davis described the shooter as a Hispanic man in his late teens to early twenties. Then, just as had happened in JJ's case, using that "trawling method," detectives took the witnesses to the precinct, where they were shown books of mug shots of people fitting that description who had been arrested in that area.

Davis couldn't identify anyone and went back to work. But it didn't take long for Sanchez to identify a suspect. Just two hours after his friend was murdered in front of him, he pointed to a picture of twenty-year-old Richard Rosario, whose mug shot was in police files because he had been arrested for—but never convicted of—a robbery. With nothing else connecting him to the crime, Richard became a suspect the same way JJ had when a witness picked his photo from a collection of mug shots.

Later that evening, Robert Davis also pointed out Richard's picture. Based on the testimony of those two witnesses, Richard was convicted of second-degree murder, and on December 17, 1998, he was sentenced to twenty-five years to life. So, what about all those alleged alibis? It was time to see Richard Rosario myself and get his side of the story.

Unlike most of the innocent people I'd done stories on, Richard was not a "model" prisoner. I learned that he'd been at many prisons, Sing Sing only one among them. It's not as though any of the other wrongfully convicted people I'd met had fully accepted the cruelty of their fate, but Richard raged against it in a way none of the others did. He acted out and wouldn't let corrections officers tell him what to do. That attitude had consequences for Richard.

For as rough as Sing Sing is, it's considered a prime location. You're close to New York City—where nearly half of incarcerated people in New York State come from—so your family can more easily get there to visit. But if you act out, you keep getting transferred farther and farther upstate. Richard wound up in nearly a dozen different facilities during his time behind bars, and he did eight years, on and off, in solitary confinement.

By the time I took the drive to visit him, Richard had been transferred further north from Sing Sing to the Sullivan County Correctional Facility, which at the time held nearly five hundred maximum-security prisoners, including serial killer David Berkowitz, the Son of Sam.

Whether it was Sing Sing or any other prison, I always felt the same way right before I went inside. People always think it's fear, but I've never really felt afraid. For me, there's always a sad, hopeless feeling that permeates a prison. Once it gets on you, it's hard to shake.

As Richard was brought into the conference room where I would interview him, my first thought was that this was a man who did more push-ups in a day than I've done in my entire life. He was all muscle. Frustration and anger seemed to be radiating off him like heat. Richard had already served twenty years, and I could see it had affected him in a way that didn't show up on David Lemus, JJ, Eric Glisson, or Johnny Hincapie. With Richard, I could see the hate. Plenty of people in prison are angry, but Richard made no attempt to hide it. It was almost as if his anger defined him, and in the months to come, I'd better understand why.

Right away there was a problem. Corrections officers were seated at a desk outside our little conference room, and Richard wanted the door closed.

"I don't want these motherfucking officers hearing my story," he said.

"They're going to hear your story," I said. "If I do my job right, the whole country will hear your story. If there's something to fix, that's how it will get fixed."

The officers wouldn't let us close the door—it was against the rules. Richard grumbled, but he let it go and we began to talk. Richard told me he didn't know Jorge Collazo, and he certainly didn't kill him. He said the first time he even heard about the murder was two weeks after the crime, in June 1996, when he was in Florida visiting friends. His mom called from the Bronx and told him the police were looking for him. "They want to talk to you about a murder," she said.

Richard said he had no idea what she was talking about and that there must have been a mix-up. He took a bus home to New York to clear up what he thought was a misunderstanding.

"I turned myself in when I heard police were looking for me," Richard told me. "I gave detectives everything they needed that first night to prove my innocence. They never investigated any of it."

That included the names, addresses, and phone numbers of thirteen people who he said could confirm he was in Florida when the shooting took place. He told me he'd thought that would be it.

"I figured they'd make a few calls, confirm my story, and I'd be released that evening," Richard told me. Instead, he was arrested for murder and hadn't been a free man since. "Do you believe I'm still here? It's insane."

Richard was twenty when he was arrested, a husband and the father of a two-year-old boy and a four-year-old girl. As I spoke with him, he was months away from turning forty. His two kids, Amanda and Richard Jr., were now adults who visited him a couple of times a year. As tough as he was, you saw him melt when he talked about them. He told me it was the kids and his wife that kept him going all these years.

"I'm gonna die on my feet fighting for my freedom, for my children," he said. "And that's what I'm going to keep doing for the rest of my life."

I'd already read through the police reports and knew that not one noted a conversation with any of the alibi witnesses Richard had provided them. What I needed to do was obvious. I had to speak with the witnesses myself.

On November 5, 2014, I headed to Florida. Glenn Garber and Rebecca Freedman, Richard's pro bono attorneys from the Exoneration Initiative, provided me with contact information for the thirteen people whose names Richard had given police the night he turned himself in nearly two decades earlier.

My first stop was Jupiter, where John and Jeanine Torres lived. They were the first two names Richard had given detectives. A police car was in their driveway. That's because John was a Palm Beach County sheriff's deputy.

Well, that's a pretty credible witness, I thought.

John was leaning against his police cruiser, still in his uniform, when I interviewed him.

"My son was born on June 20, 1996, and they're claiming that Richard killed someone June 19, 1996," Torres said. "That's physically impossible because he was in my house when we were leaving for my wife to go to the hospital. I am looking at him and talking to him June 19 and June 20. It is 1,000 percent impossible for Richard to have committed that crime because there is no way—he can't be in New York and Florida at the same time."

John explained that back then he hadn't yet become a cop; at the time he was twenty-one and unemployed. I asked him if anybody had called him the night Richard turned himself in and provided police with John's contact information.

"Not a single phone call. Not a letter. Nothing."

I also interviewed Jenine, John's wife. She told me she didn't like Richard and that she thought he was a bad influence on her husband, which is exactly why she remembered that he was in her house on June 19, 1996. How could she forget? She was going into labor, and she wanted him to leave.

"He was sitting on my sofa, and I remember telling him, 'Rich, you got to go, my baby is coming.'"

John said that after he'd heard about Richard's arrest, he took the initiative to call Richard's court-appointed lawyer but didn't hear back for more than a year. Then, shortly before the trial began, the lawyer called John and Jenine and asked them to testify. And they did. They were the only two alibi witnesses who took the stand. Apparently the jury didn't believe them.

I worked my way down the list of the other alibi witnesses, speaking with six more people on that trip, who all told me the same thing: Richard was definitely in Florida that day, and they remembered because of the baby's birth. I was struck by how several of those people didn't particularly care for Richard, so they had no reason to lie to protect him. And yet they all said the same thing.

Driving around Florida from one witness to another, I felt a rising sense of disbelief. Unlike the witnesses in JJ's case, I'm not sure you could find more credible people than these. The roster included a cop, a corrections officer, and a pastor. It felt like a bad joke.

When I got back to New York I continued to track down more people, including Irwin Silverman, the detective who initially took Richard's statement with his list of thirteen alibi witnesses the night he turned himself in. Silverman, or "Silky" as he told me to call him, was about eighty years old and long retired. He asked that we meet at his synagogue, which is where I filmed an interview with him.

Silky told me he'd been with the NYPD for forty-one years, most of that time as a detective in the Bronx. He said he didn't really remember much about Richard's case because he hadn't been the lead detective. I showed him the list of witnesses that he transcribed back then as Richard spoke. He told me that he put that list in the case file and seemed surprised when I told him no one ever followed up.

"Would it be upsetting to you if that never happened?" I asked him.

"Yeah, sure," he replied. "Why not? With that information that I got that night, I assume those people would have been spoken to. If that didn't happen, I'd feel things were left out."

I tried to speak with Richard's trial attorney. He didn't want to talk to me, even though Richard asked him to. But over the years Richard had encountered a large number of smart, dedicated lawyers who were deeply troubled by his conviction and worked for free to help him. Chief among them was Chip Loewenson. Five years after Richard's conviction, a former classmate from Yale Law School had asked Chip if he could help.

Chip told me he thought it was a slam-dunk case for an appeal.

"Once I read into the case, it was clear-cut and obvious that Richard Rosario did not get a fair trial because he didn't have effective assistance of counsel," Chip told me.

Richard had had no money, so he was assigned a court-appointed attorney—a woman named Joyce Hartsfield, who had the case for about a year before she moved on for personal reasons. Richard was then assigned a new attorney, Steven Kaiser. Chip believes that one or both attorneys screwed up in a big way.

"The first lawyer applied to the court to get expenses paid for a defense investigator to go to Florida," Chip explained. "That petition was granted, and then she didn't do anything for a year."

When the case was handed over to Kaiser, Hartsfield told him that the petition had been denied even though in fact it had been granted.

"It was just a mistake, a mix-up," Chip said.

Maybe. But what it meant was that no one fully investigated the alibis, not even Richard's own attorney.

Freeing Richard became Chip's mission, just like freeing JJ had become mine. And in 2004, six years after Richard had been sent away, Chip won Richard a rare legal victory: a new hearing in the Bronx before Judge Edward

Davidowitz. Chip represented Richard and called seven alibi witnesses to testify—including the witnesses I'd spoken with in Florida—but the judge wasn't swayed. He found that Richard's additional witnesses were "questionable and not as persuasive" as the two who testified at his trial and were discounted by the jury. And in spite of the "misunderstanding or mistake" made by Richard's attorneys, the judge found, both had represented him "with integrity," in "a thoroughly professional, competent, and dedicated fashion."

Most significant of all: the judge wrote that the people's case was "strong" and Richard's conviction was "amply supported by the evidence." The motion was denied.

After having spoken with the witnesses myself, I couldn't grasp how a judge could have listened to them and thought they were lying. *All of them?* It seemed so painfully obvious to me that the case against him was hardly a case at all. There was no physical or forensic evidence linking Richard to the crime, nor was there a motive. The entire case against him came down to two eyewitnesses, Michael Sanchez and Robert Davis, so I had to track them down.

Sanchez wouldn't talk to me, but I found an address for Davis in Brooklyn and showed up without warning at his apartment building. Davis was home, invited me in, and said I could record our conversation about what he remembered from the day of the crime.

"I'm cleaning the streets and I see three gentlemen coming towards me and two of them are having words, exchanging words," he said. "One of them is saying, 'You're not going to do this no more,' so in my mind I'm thinking it's over a girl. All of a sudden, I hear this shot, *bang!* I look up. The kid falls down to the ground."

When Detectives Gary Whitaker and Richard Martinez came to his workplace that evening with mug shots, Davis recalled that they only had two or three photos with them.

"So I pointed out the guy supposed to have done it and they said, 'Yeah, that's the guy.' So, I thought I did my job."

If true, this was a direct violation of police procedure, which calls for at least six photos in all (the suspect plus five fillers), because having only two or three photos increases the chances of an identification of the police's preferred suspect. An officer providing feedback like "You identified the suspect" is also forbidden, as it has been scientifically proven that when an officer provides confirming feedback, it can make an uncertain witness confident.[1]

I was curious what Davis would make of all those alibi witnesses who said that Richard Rosario was in Florida, not in New York committing a murder. Before I showed him a few video clips, I made it clear I wasn't trying to sway him in any way.

"I just want to emphasize for you, I am not trying to get you to say he is innocent. I'm not here to prove his innocence. I'm here to find the truth. That's all I care about."

I pressed play, and less than a minute later he looked up from my laptop and said, "That's kind of messed up if he's really an innocent person. It's really messed up. It really hurts my conscience now to see that if I did lock up an innocent person, that's kind of bad. Especially if the cops lied. Or BS'd me."

I felt like Davis had just kicked a door wide open.

"How did the cops lie?" I asked. "What did they say to you?"

"Well, if this really wasn't the man . . . and they're just bringing up anybody's picture to me," he replied.

"But that's not the cops saying it. That's you saying it."

"No," he said. "They showed me a picture and I said yes, it was him. Maybe I did make a mistake. You know, maybe that really wasn't the guy."

I pushed him. "The only people that say he did do it are you and this other guy Michael."

"And the cops sayin' he did it," Davis immediately shot back. Then he said, almost as if he was making an admission, "They said he was the guy, they did say that; the cops did tell me that. This is what I'm trying to tell you. They said you got the guy, thank you very much, and that was it."

If what Davis told me was true, the two officers had committed a tragic breach of protocol and policy. Police should never tell an eyewitness if they are "right" or "wrong."

In March 2014, Richard's new lawyers located a witness named Nicole Torres whom police interviewed on the day of the crime but who never testified at Richard's trial. According to a police report, Nicole appeared on the scene just

moments after Jorge Collazo was shot. The report described her as an imma-
terial witness who didn't see anything and didn't hear anything.

But when Rebecca Freedman, one of Richard's lawyers, spoke with Nicole
two decades after the murder, Nicole signed an affidavit swearing that the
police report was wrong. In fact, she told Rebecca, she had been right there
and saw the whole thing. The gunman. The getaway car. She even heard what
the killer said.

"She saw the killer jog up behind them and say, 'Jorge, this is for you,' before
shooting Jorge Collazo in the head once," Rebecca told me. "Then she saw
him turn around and jog to an intersection where there was a car waiting."

Rebecca said Nicole shared something else that was troubling.

"She said on the day of the crime police showed books of mug shots, and
she didn't identify," Rebecca said. Then a few weeks later, the detectives
came back, and they had a single photo of a male Hispanic, and they asked
her, "'Is this the guy? His family is saying he's in Florida.'"

If true, this was a wholly unreliable method and ridiculously suggestive, but
even so, Nicole did not identify Richard and she was never contacted again.
Based on this new information, Richard's lawyers filed a motion in Bronx Supreme Court, asking a judge to hold a hearing so that they could call witnesses.

Robert Johnson, who was serving his twenty-eighth year as the Bronx district attorney, responded to Richard's motion, writing that both eyewitnesses
"remain steadfast" that he was the gunman.

I called the Bronx DA's office, but Johnson—who had announced he wasn't
running for reelection and had just months left as DA—declined an interview.
The office did send me an email pointing out Richard's long list of unsuccessful appeals, including to the US Supreme Court.

In March 2015, Richard Rosario's motion was again denied.

In his decision, Judge Robert Sackett wrote that Richard had already had
"his day in court"—referring to that 2004 hearing where seven of his alibi witnesses testified and were rejected. Judge Sackett called that hearing "extensive"
and ruled that Richard's new motion "to vacate his conviction is denied in all
respects."

Ten months later, in January 2016, I drove back to the prison to check on
Richard and to hear how this latest denial was affecting him.

"I've been through it so many times, so my bar of expectation is so low," Richard said. "But it hurts. You know, you get denied. I'm not the only victim in this. To see my wife and kids, that's where it really pains me. I don't deserve this, but they definitely didn't deserve this. So, it's difficult."

Then, just two months after that interview with him, the case that seemed so dead suddenly had new life. With Robert Johnson's retirement, the Bronx had elected a new district attorney, Darcel Clark, who had been an appellate judge for years and, it turned out, came from the neighborhood where the murder happened.

Like Richard's attorneys, I was in touch with the DA's office from her first day on the job. I let them know we were planning on airing my twelve-part *Dateline* digital documentary series about Richard's case two months from then.

Not long afterward, investigators from the Bronx DA's office flew to Florida and finally interviewed those alibi witnesses for the first time, twenty years after Rosario gave them their names. On March 23, 2016, the same week *Dateline* released my series (we'd later turn the series into *Dateline*'s first podcast, *13 Alibis*), the DA's office agreed to vacate Richard's conviction. He walked out of the Bronx courthouse into the arms of his wife and children.

Three months later, Richard sat down with Lester Holt for an interview for an *NBC Nightly News* story. Richard, in a crisp gray suit, was seated opposite Lester, and he seemed subdued but as happy as I'd ever seen him.

Lester said that getting out was clearly the best day, but he asked Richard: "What was your worst day?"

Richard broke down and put his head in his hands. When he finally composed himself enough to speak, he said, "Every time I think about that cell."

Given what I'd learned, I had a great deal of compassion for Richard's rage. He'd been wrongly imprisoned, and he did not have JJ's "everything happens for a reason" philosophy or Eric Glisson's natural good manners or Johnny Hincapie's wide-eyed innocence. He was a tough guy whom prison had made much tougher.

Richard had lost his faith in humanity. So many people within the system had failed him. As I tried to get the truth out there, part of my motivation was that I wanted to prove to Richard that humanity was not all bad. That wasn't part of my role as a journalist, but it was crucial to me personally. And in 2016, when Richard was released from prison, I remember thinking how every time an innocent person walked free, it felt like emptying the ocean with a thimble. It was hard to fathom how many more were locked up. But both Richard and I were thinking about one of them that day. Among the first things Richard said to the crowd gathered to celebrate his first steps as a free man was: "Free Jon-Adrian Velazquez!"

21 THE YELLOW ENVELOPE

JJ'S CASE HAD BECOME an obsession. The more I saw what had been done to him, the more I felt an all-consuming rage that I couldn't let go. There was no way I was going to walk away from him. After JJ's latest appeal was denied, in 2016, I began talking with him more often, several times a week on the phone, at least, and visiting once a month or so.

"I don't know how much of this I can take," JJ said on one call. "It's been two decades. I live in a cage. I don't know what's next. Every year I say, 'You're going home. This is your year.' Every year I still don't know when I'm going home."

I was determined to help him, even if the only thing that felt available to me at the time was making his life at Sing Sing slightly more comfortable. My *Dateline* hour about JJ had aired four years earlier, but I didn't want there to be any confusion or create any standards issues for NBC, so my wife, Jocelyn, who had formed her own friendship with JJ, took it upon herself to make sure he had food, clothes, toiletries, and anything else that might make prison slightly more bearable. JJ never asked for anything, but I explained to him that Jocelyn and I would be upset if he didn't tell us what he needed.

"It's not your job," he told me.

Actually, I'd already done my job, and it hadn't gotten JJ anywhere. At this point, easing his suffering a little—making sure he had a sweater in the winter and some extra protein in his diet—was the right thing to do. But doing that barely put a dent in my increasing guilt that he was still behind bars despite what I'd uncovered.

JJ's boys were growing up into young men. Years earlier I'd given them a camera to film themselves. Not only would it help with the idea I had to document their real-life boyhood journey as they grew up, but it would also be the only way JJ could see them growing up, even if just from a distance.

JJ had once written me: "How does a father sit idle while his children are clearly suffering? How can a father accept that there is nothing he can do?"

It wasn't long before his worst fears were realized.

When Jon Jr. was sixteen, fighting got him sent for six months to Phoenix House, a juvenile facility. I went with Maria when she picked up her grandson. I'd first met Jon Jr. as a little boy in that prison visitors' lobby. Now, he was beginning to look so much like his dad. We headed to a deli to get something to eat and to chat, and Jon Jr. seemed so upbeat, telling Maria and me about the things he'd learned—organization techniques, anger management, "something called 'coping skills,'" he said.

At seventeen, he was old enough to visit his father on his own, something he'd never done before. I got permission from JJ, his son, and the prison to film their conversation. Much of it was filled with fatherly advice.

"What do you think your biggest issue is that you need help with?" JJ asked.

"Anger. Only thing is anger," Jon Jr. replied.

"Have you figured out where that anger's coming from?"

"It's just everything that I grew up with."

"Has to do with what happened with me. Right?"

"Yeah. A lot of it does. Like, I feel if you were there, it would be different."

"I know that what's happened to you is a product of what happened to me. And you have a right to be angry about that. You have a right to be upset. But we're gonna have to find a way to deal with it together."

Seeing Jon Jr. and his brother, Jacob, evolve through the years, I saw young lives warped by the absence of a father. I thought of all the parents kept from their children who shouldn't have been, and about what that means for society as a whole.

It all made me sad and furious, and that fury made me double down on finding answers for JJ and his family. But his lawyers, Bob and Celia, told me that without new, substantial evidence, it was the end of his legal road. They said there wasn't anything more they could do to help get JJ back in court or out of prison.

There was only one thing I could do—work harder. There had to be some new evidence somewhere waiting to be brought to light. At the same time, I wanted to get answers about my growing concern that the Manhattan DA's office was acting in something other than good faith. And if that was the case, could there be any recourse? Who would determine if that office needed to be investigated, and how would that happen?

When JJ's most recent motion, just asking the court to hold a hearing, was denied in 2016, I reached out to the one guy who I thought could give me some perspective, someone who'd caught a couple of Hail Mary throws in the past: my old friend from the Palladium case, who later became Eric Glisson's hero, federal gang investigator John O'Malley. By this point I'd known John for about fifteen years, and I felt lucky that I had some credibility with him. It takes a lot to gain John's trust. He'd followed my investigation into JJ's case and said he was troubled by it. And he said he wasn't surprised to hear that the Manhattan DA's office was fighting JJ so vigorously. He'd had his own issues with that office through the years.

"You know," he said, "maybe my friend Laurie might be able to give you some advice."

Laurie Korenbaum was an assistant US attorney in the Southern District of New York and had been chief of the Violent Crimes Unit. She had recently been asked by her boss to work on an initiative to look into questionable convictions in federal cases, and John asked her to talk to me.

We met for two hours, and Laurie said about four words as I walked her through all the details of JJ's case from beginning to end. But she had heard enough that she took the time to begin looking into the case on her own. After several months she even went up to Sing Sing to visit JJ and brought an investigator with her as well as something else.

JJ called me that night with surprising news. "They had a bunch of reports with them," he said, "that I never got."

Among the police reports they brought with them were the forty-four that had been withheld by prosecutor Eugene Hurley, who'd said they were irrelevant to JJ's defense. But if even one of those reports would have helped exculpate JJ, it would be a Brady violation, and grounds for a new trial.

I called Laurie, who told me that it wasn't her place to hand over the reports and that I should ask the Manhattan DA's office for them. Of course,

I'd already done that and been told I couldn't see them. So I began to work other sources, making an all-out push, and finally, on March 21, 2017, a yellow envelope arrived in my mailbox with all forty-four police reports inside.

I sat at my desk, opened the envelope, and began to read. When I reached report DD5 #93 I sat up straight. It was from a detective recounting a conversation that he'd had with the father of Derry Daniels, JJ's alleged codefendant, who pleaded guilty to duct-taping people alongside the shooter. Dated the day before JJ's name first came up, it recounted how Derry's father said his son had come over to his apartment the night before the murder with someone he owed money to. He described the man as a light-skinned Black man with braids—the exact description of the shooter that nearly all the eyewitnesses had initially given police in the hours after the murder. And he said he could identify that friend. But the next day, after Augustus Brown picked out JJ in a lineup, no one ever went to interview Daniels's father to see if JJ was that friend.

If someone had just gone to talk to Daniels's father, would he have been able to provide information about the real killer? Would he at least have been able to look at a photo of JJ and say yes or no, it was or wasn't him? Why hadn't anyone ever asked him? At the very least, shouldn't JJ have had the right to know this information?

As I was reading these reports, I couldn't stop thinking it had been four years since prosecutor Bonnie Sard and the CIU said they'd done a complete and thorough investigation into JJ's case. Why had so much—starting with this potentially key witness—never come to light back then?

About a week later, I was in Sing Sing and got permission to stop by JJ's cell to tell him the news about the yellow envelope and police report DD5 #93.

JJ's eyes filled with tears. "Why am I finding this out twenty years later?" he said. "There's no justice in the justice system. I lost twenty years of my life, man. I got five years left. I'm so numb that I can do it. People want to hold back information, perpetuate lies. I did not deserve this. My children didn't deserve this. My mother didn't deserve this. These people destroyed my life, destroyed my family. That's time I can't get back. My older son is the age I was when I went to prison. He was three years old when I left. My younger son doesn't know what it's like to wake up to a father. He was a month old. Even releasing me tomorrow won't make it right. Somebody had this information. Why was it withheld? This was not a mistake, Dan. They knew I was innocent."

JJ's lawyer Bob Gottlieb said the withheld report was a textbook definition of a Brady violation, and absolutely cause for a new trial. Someone else thought so, too: federal prosecutor Laurie Korenbaum. Since our meeting she'd become deeply concerned by JJ's conviction. "The more I looked into the details of JJ's case, I was troubled," she told me. "And then of course, when I saw DD5 #93, I was even more troubled. It was clear Brady material."

Laurie is now retired and only recently agreed to speak with me on the record for the first time about what happened after she read the police report: "I, of course, tell my supervisors about what we've found, and they speak with the Manhattan DA's office." Not long afterward, she says, she was told to stand down and stop investigating, and she thought it was because her supervisors believed her continued investigation would cause friction between the two offices.

"I don't think it was the specifics of JJ's case," she said. "It had more to do with the long-standing turf battle between the US attorney and the Manhattan DA offices. These are two of the most powerful prosecutors in the country, in walking distance of each other. I always knew it would be an uphill battle dealing with the Manhattan DA's office. When we had overlapping state and federal cases with them, their knee-jerk reaction was always adversarial."

Based on the discovery of DD5 #93, Bob Gottlieb filed a motion for a new hearing. As angry as JJ was about discovering new information after all these years, he was also enormously hopeful that this revelation, on top of everything else that had surfaced, would finally be his key to freedom. I could feel how much JJ agonized about not being with his sons. All he wanted was to get out to be a father to them again. He couldn't wait to get back into a courtroom.

Of course, that wasn't going to happen quickly. The DA's office said a new prosecutor was being assigned to the case, and they needed time to reply. It felt like an overt delay tactic. I mean, if there was a legitimate concern that a possible constitutional violation had occurred, if their only focus was true justice, wouldn't they want to deal with it quickly? Why did they need a new prosecutor? For years they'd had a whole team of lawyers reviewing JJ's case who knew every detail.

And who was the "new" prosecutor they assigned? None other than assistant DA Joel Seidemann, who a decade earlier had led the retrial of David Lemus—the innocent man who had first introduced me to JJ. Now, a decade later, here was Seidemann again, fighting to keep JJ in prison.

Six months after Bob Gottlieb brought DD5 #93 to the DA's office, Seidemann asked Judge Abraham Clott for more time to get up to speed, which would postpone the hearing by several more months. In a letter to the court, Bob opposed the request, writing, "The District Attorney has had this specific matter under consideration for more than six months. . . . A man's liberty is at stake and every day he remains incarcerated is a day without justice."

Judge Clott granted Seidemann's request for more time.

While JJ yet again was made to wait, the consequences of his absence for his family never seemed to end.

When he was eighteen, Jon Jr. had been convicted of attempted robbery and did two years in prison. Now, at twenty-three, he was out on parole and driving a delivery truck and in danger of being sent back to prison because he'd been arrested again. One night in May 2017, as her son was waiting for a new hearing, Maria called to tell me that her grandson was hiding out at a motel in Rockland County and asked if I would go see him.

I pulled up to the motel, a single strip of rooms next to a gas station. Jon Jr. let me in.

Twenty years earlier, his father, JJ, had spent the night in another depressing motel room waiting to turn himself in. The next day he had volunteered for a lineup, and that would be the end of his freedom. What was going to happen to his son Jon Jr.?

"You look so stressed, man," I said when he opened the door. The TV was on. He looked lost and began telling me about what led to his recent arrest.

"I came back from a long trip," Jon Jr. said. "Somebody called me. One of my friends had gotten robbed." He said he and his friends went to get the money back, got caught, and he was arrested for burglary. Now he was facing another prison sentence and he wanted to make a run for it.

"Have you thought this through?" I asked.

"No," he said.

"Let's start doing that now together. What are your options? Tell them to me."

"To go in. To not go."

"What happens if you go?"

"I'll be in jail."

"What's the best thing if you turn yourself in?"

"I do four months."

"And if you run? What's that look like?"

"I gotta get into the right state of mind. I can't go back in now."

"Does it feel good to live like that? On the run? Hiding?"

"I can work."

"Not if there's a warrant out for your arrest."

"There's just a lot going through my mind," he said. "I'm trying to figure out what I'm going to do."

This was the same little boy I'd met holding his grandmother's hand fifteen years earlier. Maria was beside herself, convinced she'd failed twice over, as mother to her only child and as grandmother to his two boys. But it wasn't Maria who had done this. It was clear to me it had more to do with a system that had kept a man away from his sons for their entire childhoods.

"Are you trying to be like your dad? You think he was gangster?" Maria once asked Jon Jr. "He isn't gangster. If you want to be like your father, you should be a good man, go to school, try to make your life better like he is, fight for justice."

But as I sat with him in that motel room, I knew it wasn't my place to say any of that. All I could say was that I felt so sorry for him, for the whole family, and try to be there as a voice of reason.

I told him how much his dad loved him and how difficult it must be for him. "I don't want to pretend I know what it's like for you or what the right decision is. You've got to decide that for yourself. I'm sorry you're going through this."

I gave him a hug, but I couldn't tell if I was helping at all. I headed back to my car and sat there for a few minutes. My phone rang. It was JJ calling from Sing Sing. He was worried about his son.

Jon Jr. didn't turn himself in. Months later, police caught up with him. He was sentenced to two and a half more years in prison.

Finally, on January 18, 2018, ten months after that yellow envelope full of police reports found its way to my desk, JJ was going to be back in a courtroom for the first time since he was convicted in 2000. Judge Abraham Clott, who had denied JJ's request for a hearing a few years earlier, would be the one who would determine whether DD5 #93 was "exculpatory and material."

The only other time that JJ had been outside of prison walls in nearly two decades was when he was interviewed by the prosecutors from the CIU six years earlier. He had been bitterly disappointed with the outcome back then, but now he had a lot of hope that this would finally be the tipping point that led to his freedom.

Maria bought him an outfit for the occasion. After being transported from prison, he was allowed to change his clothes in a holding cell, and with his hands shackled behind him, JJ walked into the courtroom wearing a sharp blue suit and designer glasses and with his head held high.

Bob Gottlieb was the first up, telling the judge that the new evidence was significant and should have been turned over to JJ's legal team prior to his trial. Joel Seidemann opened his argument on a surprising note. He made me an issue.

"We provided a copy of DD5 #93 to Dan Slepian prior to August 2011," Seidemann said. "He had that document. It now appears that Mr. Gottlieb in his reply-affidavit has claimed that he got that document from Dan Slepian in March of 2017."

Hearing Seidemann mention my name, I thought, *Here we go again.* Six years earlier the DA's office had brought me up during their interview with JJ, when they asked if I was footing the bill. I certainly wasn't. He had pro bono representation. And as for this new assertion, I had no idea what Seidemann was talking about. I had received documents in 2011 after filing a Freedom of Information Act request, but I hadn't seen this report in that file. I don't think the report was included, though I can't prove it now. And it doesn't make a difference. Even if they had sent me the report, why would that have mattered? I wasn't part of JJ's legal team, and the DA's office had already admitted they'd withheld it prior to trial.

Then Seidemann got to the heart of his argument—that Judge Clott could evaluate only that single sheet of paper, not everything that had already been litigated in JJ's case. In other words, if that police report had been turned over, would it likely have changed the jury's verdict? Not a chance, Seidemann said.

The hearing lasted an hour and a half, and for the first time in many years, I was optimistic that JJ would finally be vindicated and freed. That feeling didn't last very long.

Judge Abraham Clott's decision came three months later.

Denied.

Clott said that although the DA had held back that police report, the information in it "does not cast doubt on petitioner's guilt, and was not material, because there's no reasonable possibility that it would have led to a different verdict."

JJ found out about the denial in a call from his attorneys. He later told me it felt like a sword through his heart: "I thought I might be able to wear that suit and walk out one day."

I was absolutely devastated. I honestly had thought that this newly discovered evidence was the last straw. And now JJ was out of options.

I refused to give up fighting for his release, but I knew it was highly unlikely that another envelope full of documents would arrive or that I could find anything new on my own. So I started introducing JJ to other people who could advocate for him in a way I couldn't. One of them was them was my friend Jason Flom, founder of Lava Records and a founding board member of the Innocence Project. We'd met a few years earlier at a dinner party and bonded over our mutual interest in criminal justice reform.

Jason interviewed JJ for his podcast *Wrongful Conviction*. He also thought JJ would be a good candidate for clemency, a system by which a governor can grant a pardon or lessen someone's sentence. Even before Judge Clott's decision, Jason had helped JJ put together an impressive and thorough clemency application and helped lobby Governor Andrew Cuomo. During the months-long application process, JJ was even asked by the governor's office where he'd live if he got clemency, which got his hopes up yet again that he would be freed.

But in the end, disappointment. JJ was denied clemency in 2017. He was denied again in 2018, and again in 2019. With each passing year, the pressure and frustration continued to weigh on me. *What a waste*, I thought. *What a tragedy*. And then I felt guilty thinking about how I was feeling, given where JJ was. Then, as if JJ needed a reminder of the limitations and dangers of life in prison, COVID hit.

22   "US" VS. "THEM"

COVID IS PARTICULARLY FRIGHTENING in a prison, where it is impossible to socially distance, and especially in a place like Sing Sing, with a population of fifteen hundred or so men.

In early April 2020, JJ called me from the shared phone in the yard. He sounded terrible. For the first time in all the years I'd known him, I heard real fear.

I was worried about him. "Tell me. What's going on in there?"

"It's the inevitable. The numbers have changed in here."

Everyone was terrified, he said. One officer kept yelling things like, "I'm not gonna die here! I want the whole block bleached and cleaned!"

JJ said he washed his hands so often, his skin had become red and raw. He told me he was being extra cautious: he was doing walks and workouts to keep his lungs strong, and he carried a roll of tissue around his waist and didn't touch a doorknob or anything else without wrapping tissue around his hands. He told me he was thinking of making a mask out of a washcloth and shoestrings even though masking wasn't allowed in the prison for security reasons.

"I'd rather get written up for that than get sick," he said. "This virus doesn't leave room for mistakes."

His main concern was that he and the rest of the population were tense, confused, and anxious. He said, "No one knows what's happening, man. We see Cuomo on TV, but it doesn't help us. We don't know what's happening in here. The superintendent needs to talk to us more."

So I called Superintendent Capra and said I'd heard from JJ, and I thought he needed to keep the population more informed about what was happening.

"How am I going to do that?" he said.

"You have Channel 22, right?" I said, referring to Sing Sing's internal television channel that the men can watch in their cells. "I'll come over."

I showed up at the prison with masks, gloves, and a camera and filmed the superintendent sitting at a desk, two flags behind him, dressed in a suit and tie and appearing calm and in charge. He spoke about mask wearing and social distancing in the yard. He said that all programs had been canceled and that unfortunately basketball and soccer weren't allowed for the time being. He explained how all visits would be canceled for the foreseeable future, but he invited the incarcerated population to share ideas about how to make the visiting room safer whenever it did reopen. And he also reported the scary news that four men had already died from COVID and nine were in the infirmary.

"We will get through this—I'm very, very confident of that," he said. "Thank you, stay safe. I will see you all on rounds."

As things started to open up a few months into the pandemic, Jocelyn decided to have a fiftieth-birthday party for me in our backyard. She planned a special gift: a box containing a collection of photos and cards from people I'd known from all different parts of my life. When she was working on it, she asked JJ if he and maybe some of the guys I volunteered with from the Voices from Within project wanted to do a card for it.

"No, thanks," JJ told her. "We'll do our own thing."

On my birthday, I received the box from Jocelyn. Our family, friends, and coworkers had contributed memories and inside jokes. It made me laugh and cry. I could think of no better gift on earth than that. Then the other box arrived.

It was covered with dozens of small gray rocks—each one harvested from the prison yard at Sing Sing. The top opened to reveal an inlaid mirror. A drawer in the front pulled out. Inside was a group photo of the whole crew there in their prison greens. Underneath the photo were index cards with notes written by each of them in careful penmanship.

As I marveled at what they'd sent, the phone rang. JJ had gotten the entire Voices from Within group to line up in the prison yard. Each one took a turn to wish me happy birthday and then passed the phone to the next guy.

In that moment, I had a dozen friends drinking beer on my deck, but I sat there in my office listening with tears in my eyes as each man excitedly shared his contribution to the box. I told them the truth, that it was an object of beauty, and it had clearly taken an incredible amount of hard work to assemble. I told them it was the best gift I'd ever received, and I meant it.

I haven't shared the box with many people. It feels so personal. But I think there's value in hearing how much gratitude and strength can be created by the smallest gestures of attention and respect. Here are just a few of the notes inside:

> You give the buried voice sound. You share the wisdom from incarcerated persons who have a story to tell that others can learn from.

> I am more than my current circumstances. I am a father, a brother, a friend, a man, and an important member of my society. Thank you, Dan, for being you and believing in me.

> Thank you for allowing me to perform my duties as a human being.

Javier Miranda, the talented craftsman who assembled the box, wrote:

> Rocks in the dirt will remain just that, rocks in the dirt, without a builder. Rock by rock you have built something greater. By giving us purpose and a voice, you have created something that will stand the test of time. . . . You have become not only a builder, but also a lantern, lighting up even the darkest places in our society. Thank you for caring and sharing your life with us.

What I couldn't stop thinking about as I looked at those cards was this: There were twenty cards in that box, twenty voices on the phone. There are two million people in prison. I was at my own birthday party, and I was hardly present. It was impossible not to spend that night with one eye on that box, thinking about all the prisons with their yards full of rocks and their cells full of human beings with stories to tell.

Like most law-abiding citizens, I'd spent a lot of my life believing that I'd never be one of "those people." And then something happened to me recently that made me realize how close we all are to becoming one of "them."

One night I went out to run a quick errand in my suburban Westchester town. On the way to the store, on a road with no lights, a car swerved into my lane. I skidded, lost control of the car, went off the road, and felt myself driving through a fence. The front of the car was crushed, but I was going slow enough that the airbags didn't deploy, no glass was broken, and I wasn't hurt.

I staggered out of the car. The homeowner who saw it called 911 and ran over to check on me.

He asked me how I was. I could barely speak. I was in shock. It had been twenty years since I'd even had a fender bender, and that was when I was driving hundreds of miles a week. How could I have had an accident in my own neighborhood?

We stood there staring at the car. Soon there were three state troopers with us, the lights of their vehicles flashing. Jocelyn, whom I'd texted, arrived too. I was embarrassed. I saw other drivers looking at me as they slowly passed by. "He's acting weird. He might be drunk," I later learned the homeowner told the cops.

Suddenly there were flashlights shining in my face. Earlier that day at brunch I'd had a Bloody Mary, and I started to worry that it would show up on a Breathalyzer test. When the troopers suggested I take one, I said maybe I should call my lawyer. They said that was my right but that if I did that, they would suspend my license for 150 days. I was nervous, but I agreed to the test, and blew into the tube.

If you have a blood alcohol content of .05 to .08, in New York that's a DWAI (driving while ability impaired). Over .08 is a DWI (driving while intoxicated). Mine was .01. As soon as that number came back, the troopers' shoulders dropped. They were suddenly friendly. I wasn't even given a ticket.

"You did nothing wrong," one cop said to me, smiling. "Just bad weather, that's all."

We were all relieved that was the case. It was just a rainy night, a slick road, an overcorrection with the wheel.

But what if I'd had three Bloody Marys at brunch, or a beer that afternoon while watching TV just before I left? If behind that fence a child had been playing in a puddle? What if in that split second I'd taken a life? I'd have been in prison, potentially looking at twenty-five to life. That doesn't make me a bad person. But that still would have been the weekend that society went from considering me someone with a right to humane treatment to someone on the other side of an invisible line of decency, someone who deserved whatever I got.

How we treat incarcerated people in this country came into even sharper focus for me in 2018, when I was invited by the Vera Institute of Justice to tour Norwegian and German prisons to learn how differently those countries think about crime and incarceration. I knew, intellectually, the difference between what happens there and here—recidivism rates are lower. But what I saw affected me viscerally. There are two words that define the prison population in both of those countries: human dignity. After the Holocaust, the rights of prisoners were actually written into the German constitution. And you feel that when you're inside.

American corrections officers deal with so much violence, people who are out to get them, who come at them with homemade weapons, who throw feces. The system from start to finish is very much about "us" versus "them," and plenty of people on both sides play their part. In the late 1990s, I produced a story about a jail in Texas where corrections officers used vicious dogs to maintain order. For decades at least a few prisons have authorized the use of dogs to attack incarcerated people who won't voluntarily leave their cells.[1]

In Germany and Norway, corrections officers as well as police are trained in social work. A good day for them is making sure somebody doesn't come back to prison. A good day for an officer here is going home alive. There, the incarcerated population has to take job training. Here, you're extremely lucky to get it. There, you have to be in school. Here, it's a perk if it's even offered. There, everyone at the prison grows and eats fresh food. Here, all the food is packaged and processed. There, you wear your own clothes, and you have a door that closes. Here, you get your head shaved, you're put in a uniform, and you have no privacy whatsoever.

I came back from that trip on fire, thoughtful about how much my perspective on criminal justice in this country had changed. I used to have so much faith in the system. Now I understand that by every metric, we're making things worse.

We know there are alarmingly high recidivism rates among people who are released from prison. In one study, the Bureau of Justice Statistics tracked 404,638 people in thirty states after their release from prison and found that nearly an astonishing 76 percent were rearrested within five years.

It's not hard to see why. Reentering society isn't easy once you've been branded a felon. Formerly incarcerated people encounter a plethora of obstacles upon release, including tens of thousands of regulations around the country that affect crucial things like where they can live and work, and whether or not they can vote.[2]

As Equal Justice Initiative executive director and law professor Bryan Stevenson says, "Each of us is worth more than the worst thing we've ever done."[3]

We need to set returning citizens up for success, which means providing more education and opportunity through vocational training while they're serving their time.

I understand why most people don't care if prisoners are uncomfortable or don't get an education. It makes sense for someone working two jobs at minimum wage, struggling to get by, to say, "I'm working my ass off to send my kid to college and I'm going to give free education with my taxpayer dollars to murderers and rapists?"

How can you argue with that? But I do. Not only for the sake of those locked up, but for all of society, as well.

Studies have shown that there is a 43 percent reduction in recidivism rates for those prisoners who participate in prison education programs. Much the way water puts out fire, education puts out crime. The higher the degree, the lower the recidivism rate: 14 percent for those who obtain an associate's degree, 5.6 percent for those who obtain a bachelor's degree, and virtually 0 percent for those with a master's, a degree that is offered at only a handful of prisons in the United States.

So why do only a small percentage of prisons offer education programs? As NYU professor Rachel Barkow wrote in her insightful book *Prisoners of Politics*, "Anyone truly interested in public safety has to pay attention to the relevant empirical facts and not simply rely on gut instinct."[4]

We need to look at this issue objectively, not emotionally. I've interviewed many people convicted of crimes and, yes, some seemed to me to be beyond redemption. I believed they should be locked up forever. I'll sleep better knowing they'll never get out. But the vast majority of people who go into prison are good people who made terribly bad choices when they were young. What's more, whether we like it or not, 95 percent of all incarcerated people will be released and return into our communities.[5] Do we want those returning citizens to be educated or have learned a trade, or uneducated and full of rage?

Putting aside the broader philosophy of humane incarceration, we can surely agree that an *innocent* person shouldn't be in prison. We know that certain reforms to the system can help lower the probability of a wrongful conviction, but progress has been slow, and accountability is almost nonexistent. Prosecutorial misconduct is often a cause of a wrongful conviction, but rarely, if ever, has a prosecutor been held accountable for holding back information or prosecuting an innocent person in bad faith.

After my fiftieth birthday, another whole year passed with no new hope for JJ. COVID waves came and went. I turned fifty-one. Casey started college. Work went on as ever. I got a couple of shows on the air. I was nominated for Emmys and didn't win them. But finally—*finally*—I got the call I'd been hoping for.

23　"YOU'RE BEING TRANSFERRED"

ON THE MORNING OF August 17, 2021, I was sitting in my home office when my phone rang. It was Superintendent Capra, and he got right to the point. JJ had just received clemency from Governor Cuomo. He was about to tell JJ he was going home. He thought I should know.

"Wait for me! Wait for me!" I yelled into the phone as I grabbed my camera and ran out the door with my shoelaces flapping, my shirt half on, batteries flying everywhere. I was at Sing Sing in record time.

That JJ got clemency was a miracle. It's granted only in extremely rare circumstances. The New York State constitution allows the governor to grant it to people who have been convicted of state crimes, and in two forms: a commutation, which shortens a sentence—what Cuomo gave JJ—or a pardon, which removes some or all of the consequences of a conviction. To be considered means submitting an extensive application to the Executive Clemency Bureau, part of the Department of Corrections.

JJ had applied before but was denied each time. Finally, though, at the eleventh hour, here it was: mercy. Why now? Only Andrew Cuomo can explain why it was one of his last acts in office before he had to resign over allegations of sexual harassment.

After spending more than twenty-three years in that tiny cell at Sing Sing, JJ was going to be free. He'd be able to hug his mother and his children. He'd be able to sleep in a bed softer than a board. He'd get to eat fresh food and swim in the ocean. He could be a human being in the world.

Superintendent Capra was beaming when I arrived, so excited was he to be the one to deliver the good news. We walked together down the concrete hallways to honor block and up to JJ's cell on the second tier, my camera rolling the whole time.

"You've been transferred," Capra told JJ in his best deadpan voice.

"Where?" JJ said, looking alarmed.

Capra, a born performer, read from the paper in front of him. "Haverstraw, New York. You know where that is?"

JJ suddenly realized where he was being sent—to his mother's.

"You've been granted clemency," Capra said.

Violating all protocols, the two men wrapped their arms around each other and hugged.

As word of what had just happened spread through the cell block, the entire unit erupted in deafening applause. This man—who'd helped free so many others, who'd written letters for them and helped them research their cases, who'd found so many ways big and small to make that horrible place a little kinder and to give the most desperate people hope—was going home. He wouldn't walk free for another three weeks, so he spent that time saying goodbye and giving away his things for the last time after years of premature farewells.

Finally, on September 9, 2021, the day arrived when the huge metal door to the prison would slowly slide open and Jon-Adrian Velazquez would walk out, a purple mesh bag of law books and some personal items over his shoulder. I met him early in the morning at his soon-to-be-vacant cell and interviewed him before he was processed out. Cuomo had commuted his sentence, allowing him to go home early, but hadn't issued him a pardon. While he would be physically free and assured that his years of incarceration were really over, he would still officially be a convicted killer.

"Today, I will finally step foot out of prison," JJ said. "I practically grew up in prison. I've been answering to a number: 00A2303. That was my identity for the last twenty-four years. That meant more than my name."

I asked him whether living in a cell by himself for more than two decades had led him to believe his suffering had been for some higher purpose.

"I've gone beyond belief," he replied. "I realized that that's the only thing that makes sense to say that this was my training ground. To know is to experience, so I had to experience this so that I can try to work on changing this. Right?"

Emotion overwhelmed me.

When JJ started writing those "Dear Mr. Slepian" letters to me in 2002, I had no idea we'd be in this together for more than two decades. From time to time since that day I've revisited my box of JJ's letters, but I can't get through more than a few at a time. They are heartbreaking.

As my own daughter grew up, I felt even more acutely the depth of the pain suffered by JJ and by all those separated from their children. People in prison described to me the agony of not being able to work to protect their kids, to do things for them as small as making them pancakes in the morning or as large as keeping them out of trouble in a rough neighborhood.

I met JJ when he was a young father. He got out when he was forty-five.

"I want to tell you something before we leave," I said. "You know, I met you before I met my daughter. The year before she was born. And I took her to college two weeks ago. And there's a certain irony to that, for me. It's like the end of a chapter and the beginning of a new one." I started to cry. "My friendship with you is one of the most important relationships in my life."

"Absolutely," JJ said as we hugged. "You are family."

"Family," I repeated. Then, wiping away tears, I perked up. "Do you want to go home?"

"Yes, I want to go home."

"Let's go home," I said.

My camera crew followed JJ as he left honor block, saying goodbye to all the men he was leaving behind.

Waiting for him outside were his mother and his two boys. Maria held him tightly for a long time, wailing, as if she couldn't believe he was real. It's a sound I will never be able to forget. It was guttural, full of excruciating pain and overwhelming joy.

I spent the rest of the day with JJ, and I served as his chauffeur over the next few days of his freedom as he began to rebuild his life. He was mandated to register, in person, with the parole office within twenty-four hours of his release. He needed an ID, a toothbrush, a bed. But while I was thrilled for him, I realized that I didn't feel the way I had long anticipated I would. What I felt was guilt that it had taken so long for the day to come. The decades had taken a toll on me.

"You never feel like it's enough," Jocelyn said, leaning in the doorway of my office one day after JJ's release. "There was no joy in you when JJ got out. You were nothing but remorseful that it took so long. You couldn't even take a minute to be glad."

How could I when JJ was still a convicted killer in the eyes of the law? And when the emotional wreckage was everywhere?

Soon after his release, JJ did something I'd never have imagined anyone was strong enough to do: he returned to Sing Sing—after spending nearly twenty-four years behind bars—this time as a volunteer. He'd promised the men of Voices from Within he'd be back to help, and he kept his promise.

He also quickly landed a job, one that would continue to bring him inside prisons across the country. JJ was hired to be the program director for a non-profit called the Frederick Douglass Project for Justice, which organizes prison visits to facilitate structured meetings and conversations between members of free society and prisoners, so that they can learn from each other, form powerful connections, and understand their shared humanity. The project was launched by my close friend Marc Howard, a professor at Georgetown University and founder of the school's Prisons and Justice Initiative.

For most of their childhoods, JJ's children didn't get to live with their father. But now he was back at home with them, trying to make up for all the lost time. And he became a grandfather too. In July 2022 Jon Jr. had twin daughters, and in September 2023 Jacob became a father, as well. JJ was there to marvel at his sons' children and to tease Maria for how many bows she'd bought for the babies' hair.

"Mom, they don't even have any hair yet!" JJ said.

"But they *will*," she replied.

JJ's new life was far from normal. As a middle-aged grandfather, he had a 9:00 p.m. curfew. He was required to check in with his parole officer regularly, and he needed a letter anytime he traveled out of state, even to go to the White House and meet with the president of the United States.

In October 2022, a year after he was freed, that's what he did. JJ was invited by NowThis News to be one of a handful of participants to sit across from President Biden for a panel to discuss pressing societal issues, including criminal legal reform.[1] When it was JJ's turn to ask a question, he said to the president: "How can we create clear uniform standards for clemency so that incarcerated people are motivated to change, and know what they need to accomplish to show that they're ready to return to their families and communities?"

"First of all," President Biden replied, "on behalf of all society, I apologize for it. I mean, twenty-three years—my God."

"Thank you, Mr. President," JJ said.

Then Biden told a story about the time he'd met with Nelson Mandela when he came to Washington after he'd been released from prison and become president of South Africa. "How can you not hate?" Biden remembered saying to Mandela. And he recalled Mandela's response: "The jailers were just doing their job. Just doing what they were paid to do. And as I left, they said, 'Good luck, Nelson.'" At that point the president, overcome, said to JJ: "I admire the hell out of you."

That was the president speaking. But the president has no authority to pardon JJ, because he was convicted of a state crime, not a federal one. Until a New York judge exonerates JJ—something that could happen tomorrow or never—he will continue to remain, in the eyes of New York State, a convicted killer. It seems outrageous because it is outrageous, but it's shocking only for people who don't understand the system. For those of us who've been covering these things, JJ's legal status is par for the course.

He hopes that will change soon.

Nearly all the men whose stories I've told in this book received compensation for the years stolen from them. Ultimately, Eric Glisson and the Bronx Six were awarded a combined $40 million in restitution for having spent more than seventeen years in prison—only a bit shy of the $40.7 million settlement to the five wrongfully convicted men in the Central Park jogger case.

On the one-year anniversary of his release, Eric Glisson opened a juice bar in the Bronx that he called Fresh Take, because of his new chance at life. He built it himself. He also bought Sasino, a water company in the Dominican Republic.

In a civil suit against the police for coercing his confession, Johnny Hincapie, by then fifty years old, received $18 million from the City of New York.

He moved to Florida and had two children. As he was nearing an age when many men retire, his life could finally begin.

After his release, Richard Rosario sued the city. It took six years for him to go to trial. Finally, in the summer of 2022, he had his day in court. I was there every day, watching the whole thing. In the end, he was awarded $5 million.

The City of New York eventually settled a lawsuit with David Lemus for $1.25 million and with Olmedo Hidalgo for $2.2 million. They took a settlements as fast as they could, before there were even depositions. Lemus would go on to have three children in the years after he was exonerated. The first, David Jr., was born on Christmas Day. Lemus now works at a car dealership.

Nationwide, as of a year ago, $2.65 billion had been paid out to exonerated people bringing civil rights suits, with an average payout of $3.7 million, or $318,000 for each year spent incarcerated.[2] Still, I feel it has to be said: Money does not fix this level of injustice. It doesn't restore the best years of a life. If you missed out on having a family, or on being there for your children their whole childhoods, or had to go two decades without being held by someone who loved you—how does money make up for that?

I thought I knew everything there was to know about these cases. Then, while I was writing this book, came one more surprise.

24 "WE RUINED THIS PERSON'S LIFE"

WHEN I WAS MAKING some calls to do due diligence for this book, I tried getting in touch with Bonnie Sard of the Conviction Integrity Unit, Cyrus Vance, and various other people who hadn't wanted to talk to me on the record over the years. Sard still wouldn't talk to me on the record, and neither would Vance. But there was someone who was willing to speak with me: another juror in JJ's trial. I'd reached out to her years earlier and she hadn't wanted to do an interview. Now, she was finally ready to talk. "I need to do this," she said.

On a cold morning a few days later, I drove to Long Island for the interview. As soon as we saw each other, she burst into tears. She told me that during JJ's trial, she thought the eyewitness evidence against him was shaky and that he was innocent. When deliberations began, several other jurors agreed with her, but most were adamant that JJ was guilty. The fact that an ex-cop had been shot added pressure, as did the fact that none of them could go home until they reached a verdict.

"We were sequestered," the juror told me. "We were in this terrible hotel near LaGuardia Airport. I didn't sleep. It was terrible."

The jury deliberated for three full days.

"It was so tense inside that room," the juror said, "especially as the days passed. People were tired and arguing. Everyone just wanted to get out of there."

She explained how one by one the jurors who first voted not guilty began to flip, and that on the third day of deliberations, she did too. It was right before Halloween. Jurors said they just wanted to see their kids.

"And you felt that he was not guilty even when you voted guilty?" I asked.

"I did, I'm sorry to say. I should have stood my ground, but I didn't. I succumbed to the pressure. I'm a terrible human being, I think."

In 2001, the law in New York State changed, so it's no longer mandatory to sequester a jury in criminal cases.[1] Maybe if JJ had been arrested after that change, his trial would have ended differently. This juror said she thought so.

"I should have held my ground," she said. "I didn't do it. I pray that no one I ever know has to go through that, being incarcerated for something they didn't do. People should understand the magnitude of the responsibility, making a judgment on someone's life."

She said she never wanted to serve on a jury again and became emotional describing how it felt when the guilty verdict was read: "I started crying. I'm going to start crying again."

And she did.

"As we left the courtroom, the judge saw me and another juror upset. He pulled us into his chambers. He wanted us to take a breath. It was a horrible experience. My gut said I did the wrong thing. This young kid! We realized we ruined this person's life."

In the years since then, she's thought of JJ often and googled him many times. Every time she drove upstate she'd think about visiting him at Sing Sing, to tell him she was sorry. She kept that obsession a secret from everyone she knew, even from her husband.

I shared with her that JJ was making a difference in the world now, that he'd even met with President Biden. As terrible as the past two decades had been, I told her, "he never would have been in the Oval Office without going through that."

"Well, it's a big price to pay," the juror said. "I'm sorry that I wasn't strong enough to defend him. I didn't treat him like he was part of my family. I would do anything to protect my family. I went with the majority rule, and I shouldn't have done that. I didn't have the strength to do what I should have done. I'm very ashamed of myself. I apologize to his mother and his children."

She kept crying, and so I finally said: "If I can be so arrogant as to say what I think JJ would tell you right now, I would say the first thing JJ would say is that he would never condone the injustice that happened to him. He would never wish it on anyone, that it was hell, and if he could do it all over again, he obviously wouldn't want to have to live through that experience. Having said that, he also believes that everything happens for a reason. The reality is, what he will tell you is that his lived experience got him where he is today, and that you were part of it." I said that to make her feel better, but I also believe it to be true.

"The fact that he was able to see the world the way he did and had to endure that suffering for as long as he did gives him the tools to be able to help so many other people. Had you not done what you did, Richard Rosario would be in prison. Eric Glisson might be in prison. He would not have led me to all of those people. He would not have had the consciousness to start Voices from Within, potentially helping hundreds or thousands of at-risk kids make better choices. He wouldn't be working for the Frederick Douglass Project.

"I don't think JJ was violent, but he was certainly selling drugs. He was a young dad, and he was in the streets, and he needed something. He certainly didn't need twenty-four years in prison, but he just met with the president of the United States in part because of you."

I told her she changed my life, too. What she did was wrong, but if she'd done right, who knows how everyone's life would have gone? I told her that without her, "JJ wouldn't be my brother. You changed my life. You brought us together. That's the other side of it. It happened because it had to happen, because it was meant to happen. That's how I feel about it. I can't prove it, but that's what I believe, and I think that's what JJ believes, too."

I went on to say that speaking to me, helping me add context to JJ's story, was her opportunity to make a different choice now than she made then. She didn't speak up for him the first time; now she has. She wasn't brave before, but now she was.

The interview left me shaken. Talking to that juror made me think about who is serving on juries and how many must feel similar pressure. When we talk about eyewitness misidentification, police and prosecutorial misconduct, false confessions, Brady violations, ineffective assistance and counsel for the indigent, we also must talk about the enormous role and responsibility every one of us plays in the system.

It's not that I don't believe in humanity. I do. But I also think that we'd all like to believe that we're better than we are. We'd all like to believe that on a jury we wouldn't be the person who says, "Let's just get out of here and go home." We'd like to believe that we'd never make a false confession. We'd never be the eyewitness who identified the wrong person. We wouldn't be those people. But how do we know?

Most prosecutors, for their part, would say, "I would never lock up an innocent person."

But it's baked into the system. Detectives feel they need to solve the case and make an arrest. It's a prosecutor's job to make sure justice is done, but too often prosecutors are evaluated by their conviction rates, so they think, *I need to be tough. I need to lock people up. That's how they're going to know I'm a good prosecutor.* It's the way the system is constructed to subtly and not so subtly encourage people with great responsibilities to act irresponsibly in a way that all too often leads to tragic consequences.

One recent night I was up late, as usual, sifting through old paperwork in JJ's case. I came across a handwritten note from the lead detective, Joseph LiTrenta, from the day JJ was identified out of eighteen hundred mug shots by a witness who had ten bags of heroin sitting in front of him.

After LiTrenta got that ID, he jotted down Maria's name and ID'd her as "perp's mother." I looked at the paper and realized he was already calling JJ a "perp" without any other information. He had nothing. To me, that scrap of paper was a perfect example of the tunnel vision that leads to tragedy.

Still, I do believe that with enough patience and work and struggle, justice can prevail.

In November 2020, Manhattan voters elected Alvin Bragg as their new district attorney to replace Cyrus Vance. When Bragg was campaigning, among his top issues was the problem of wrongful convictions. He called Vance's CIU a CRINO—"conviction review in name only." When Bragg won, he disbanded Vance's CIU and started over, claiming that such investigations were a "significant priority" for the office.[2]

His new Post-Conviction Justice Unit has a website with a straightforward application for case review. And the new head of the PCJU is someone who worked for years at Legal Aid, a defense organization. JJ's conviction was among the first cases the new PCJU chose to reinvestigate. Nearly three years after JJ's release, as this book goes to press, a decision is expected any day.

Not long ago, I was asked to moderate a panel at the Innocence Conference in Phoenix. There were about three hundred exonerees in that room; taken together, they'd had more than 5,500 years stolen from them, at an obscene moral and financial cost to all of us.

Standing on the stage, I asked the room, "How many of you have been a victim of a constitutional violation?" A few hundred people raised their hands, several yelling out things like "How about four violations?"

Then I asked how many of the police or prosecutors who committed those constitutional violations were punished or held to account in any way. The room went silent. Not a single hand went up.

This journey I've been on for more than two decades began with my experience with the Palladium case. I was curious one day, and looked up the word *palladium*. One meaning of the word is a silver-white metal. Another is a statue that the Trojans considered a source of protection. The word also has a third meaning: safeguard.

Where do we find a genuine safeguard against injustice?

The stain on the moral fabric of our society left by wrongful convictions and false imprisonments is the product of more than just incompetent or malevolent police and prosecutors; it's a failure of our collective will to hold people in power accountable. We need to see these cases as fundamental injustices we all must work to correct and prevent.

When it comes to judging our fellow citizens of anything, much less a capital crime, we should ask far more questions than are typically asked. And we should ask even more questions if we're a reporter or detective or lawyer—and certainly if we're a juror with someone's life in our hands.

Hopefully one day we will look back on this era as a dark chapter in our history that we had the courage to end.

The safeguard, in other words, is us.

ACKNOWLEDGMENTS

Gratitude pours from the depth of my soul to so many extraordinary people who have helped shape my life and this book.

First, a heartfelt tribute to my mother, Myrna, my eternal supporter and first editor. Her and my sisters' unwavering belief in me throughout my life got me here. Dad, your spirit and presence resonate with me every day. To my stepmom, Carol, what a journey it's been. Bernie and John, thank you for giving me my wife, and I love how much you love Casey. Jess and Lele, thank you for standing by me.

Ada Calhoun, your collaboration, insight, and patience were pivotal to the creation of this book. My incredibly kind and brilliant editor, Bill Hamilton, publisher Deb Futter, and the Celadon team, along with my literary agents, Larry Weissman and Sascha Alper, I appreciate you taking a chance on a first-time author and giving these stories a platform they desperately deserve and need. Frances Sayers, your production editing, guidance, and attention to detail were critical and enormously helpful.

Deep respect and love to the men profiled in this book and their families—they entrusted me with deeply personal experiences. I stand in awe of you all and hope I've done you justice. You are living testaments to the extraordinary strength it takes to fight a broken system.

David Lemus, Nilsa, and Olmedo Hidalgo, you were the spark that ignited an inferno. JJ Velazquez, you are the soul of this book and no words suffice to describe what the depth of our connection means to me. Quantum entanglement brought you Geri, an extraordinary human. Maria, you are among the strongest people I've met. Jon Jr. and Jacob, you are living proof of the intergenerational toll of a heartless system, and I couldn't be more proud of how you both endured.

Eric Glisson, you are a brother to me and a loving father to your beautiful daughters. Your infectious optimism is magical. Johnny Hincapie, you survived your twenty-five-year ordeal with dignity and grace, along with your beautiful family, Maria, Carlos, and Alex. Richard Rosario suffered an unthinkable and infuriating injustice, and his family, Minerva, Amanda, and Richard Jr., remained strong and elegant throughout their nightmare.

Detective Bobby Addolorato, you are the catalyst of it all. More than two decades ago you introduced me to a pathological system I never before knew existed. You are a true hero. John Schwartz, thank you for allowing a young reporter to shadow you and for being so honest in front of a rolling camera. Steve Cohen, you are a brilliant lawyer and leader. I've learned so much from you. John O'Malley, you are extraordinary, and I'm proud to be your friend.

Rob Allen, my collaborator for two decades, your meticulous work on every story in this book and your selfless dedication have left an indelible mark. I love you. Eric will never be forgotten.

I am eternally grateful to so many who were instrumental in my career. Aimee Leone played an early role in launching my path. Pat McMillen, the former executive producer of *Donahue*, provided my first real job in TV. Working for Phil, an incredibly generous and kind man, was a dream come true. I met one of my closest friends there, David Scott. Carpe diem.

Since 1996, *Dateline* has been my home. Elena Nachmanoff, thank you for helping me get there. My first mentor, Bruce Hagan, died tragically in 1998, and I will never forget his generous guidance. Neal Shapiro, you are a visionary leader and a kind soul. Thank you for believing in me, and for the Yankees games. David Corvo, you have consistently elevated my stories. Liz Cole, none of this happens without your leadership at *Dateline* and NBC News Studios. Thank you for supporting the work I love and elevating it all beyond anything I could have imagined. Jim Gerety, you have always been my part-time therapist and helped me navigate a complex bureaucracy.

Adam Gorfain, your support and collaboration from the beginning was pivotal. Allan Maraynes, learning from you was like being a young ballplayer coached by Babe Ruth. Nearly every story in this book began under your direction. Paul Ryan, I cherish you as a friend, a colleague, and a fellow White Plains High School alum (despite learning you are John's brother.) Susan

Nalle, the glue that holds everything together, thank you for your immense contributions to my work and to the show over the years.

Kim Ferdinando, you are a brilliant, creative, and trusted leader. I'm proud to work with you. Lauren Capps, Sadie Bass, and Rosie Walunas, your dedication and patience are so deeply appreciated. Alex Pilkington, you are the best professor in the basement.

Preeti Varathan, our podcast, *Letters from Sing Sing*, is as much yours as mine. Nick McElroy, you are a superstar. Thanks for checking and double-checking every fact in this book.

There are so many former and current colleagues at NBC who have contributed in some way to the stories in this book and others who have simply supported me for decades, including Justin Balding, Stefani Barber, Andy Berg, Chad Bergacs, Frank Bido, Katie Blum, Liz Brown, Rob Buchanan, Bruce Burger, Evan Burgos, Loren Burlando, Andrea Canning, Tess Capodice, Justin Cece, Cate Cetta, Jared Crawford, Alexa Danner, Brad Davis, Toni DeAztlan, Molli Derosa, Dominique Donahue, Michelle Feuer, Elizabeth Fischer, ML Flynn, Veronica Fulton, Anthony Galloway, Mario Garcia, Charmian Gilmartin, David Gelles, Chris Glorioso, Tim Gorin, Rich Greenberg, Marianne Haggerty, Chris Hansen, Izhar Harpaz, Andrew Hongo, Lai-Ling Jew, Lynn Keller, Julie Kim, Dana Klinghoffer, Mary Lockhart, Josh Mankiewicz, Ellen Mason, Lauren Miller, Keith Morrison, Mike Nardi, Tommy Nguyen, Allison Orr, Miranda Patterson, Stone Phillips, Rich Platt, Meghan Rafferty, Justin Ratchford, Billy Ray, John Reiss, Adriana Ricciuto, Jim Rosenfield, Luke Russert, Tim Sandler, Andrew Siff, David Sternlicht, Mike Tabbi, Ramón Taylor, Sarah Teicher, Tim Uehlinger, Adam Wald, Ali Zelenko, and Sally Zhang.

Adam Miller, Hilary Smith, and Jen Friedman, I am so humbled by your support and attention. Jacob Soboroff, much love for your kindness and guidance; it was enormously helpful. Kim Cornett, I cherish our friendship and years of collaboration on Lester's stories.

To the men of Voices from Within: JJ, Kenyatta Hughes, Colin Absolam, Lawrence Bartley, Dario Peña, Julian Castillo, Laron Rogers, Andre Jenkins, Sean Kyler, Jermaine Archer, Markey Coleman, Brian Johnson, Bruce Bryan, Gary Benloss, Hector Roman, Steph Brathwaite, Javier Miranda, Wilfredo Laracunte, Martin Garcia, Michael Hoffler, Chris O'Neill, Bill Walsh, Jose Pérez, and so many others—thank you for including me in your world. You've all taught me so much. Rich White and Rick Albright, your selfless contributions have changed lives.

Lorenzo Johnson, Jeff Deskovic, Eric Riddick, Jabbar Collins, and Walter Ogrod, you've all survived the unthinkable. I'm grateful for our friendship.

To the former and current New York State Department of Corrections and Community Supervision team: Commissioner Dan Martuscello, Anthony Annucci, Tom Mailey, and Linda Foglia, I appreciate your flexibility and trust. Superintendent Michael Capra, you and Jackie are family. Mary Buono, you are a saint.

Peter Stern, it's impossible not to adore you and Gloria. Your selfless work is your superpower and it inspires me. Barry Scheck, you are a legend, and I'm honored to be your friend. Jason Flom, your dedication to justice is unstoppable. Khaliah Ali, thanks for keeping him grounded. Nick Turner, you were right: the trip to Germany and Norway with Vera changed my life, a trip that wouldn't have happened without Mike Novogratz's passion for justice. Scott and Christa Semple, your beautiful son Matthew's spirit lives on; he was the reason that "Justice for All" happened. Seth Smith, a great leader takes risks. Thank you for taking one on me. I hope you agree that it paid off.

Corey Kilgannon, this book would not have happened without you. Rebecca Brown, your suggestions have been invaluable, but your friendship means so much more. Sean Pica, you've changed more lives than anyone I know. Dylan Wood, your support has been constant and has never gone unnoticed. Mara Burros-Sandler, M. Quentin Williams, and Dave Joachim, thank you for your friendship and care.

I've encountered many attorneys along this journey who have fought for the innocent, including Peter Cross, Bob Gottlieb, Ron Kuby, Chip Loewenson, Steve Zeidman, Rachel Barkow, Patricia Cummings, Earl Ward, Jonathan Abady, Julia Kuan, Oscar Michelan, Tom Hoffman, Glenn Garber, and Rebecca Freedman. The system needs more lawyers like you.

Celia Gordon, I appreciate our connection, even though you've become closer to my wife than me, but at least I have Roy. Sean Gallagher, your talent and patience have finally paid off. Thank you for sticking with me.

To the Stabiles and the Brucheys, I'm enormously grateful for our decades of enduring friendship. Jen Dembo, care and kindness define you. Marc Howard, you are not just a friend but a brother from another mother. I look forward to the adventures that lie ahead.

Desiree Perez, Dania Diaz, TeamRoc, and the United Justice Coalition, thank you for caring so much and for all you do for so many people.

Meek Mill, it was an honor to witness you walking out of prison. Michael Rubin, I'll never forget your kindness in letting me tag along.

Dawn Porter, I'm so grateful that you've dedicated your immense talent to creating a docuseries about these cases.

Most of all, Lester Holt, my dear friend, you are the unsung hero for so many people, including me. Your quiet leadership, kindness, and humanity are a gift to all those who know and work with you.

And to Jocelyn and Casey: none of this would be possible without you.

NOTES

INTRODUCTION

1. You may notice that I avoid using the word *inmate* anywhere in this book. This is deliberate. Words are powerful, and language matters. Dehumanizing labels form stereotypes and stigmas. For further reading on the subject, see Erica Bryant's 2021 article "Words Matter: Don't Call People Felons, Convicts, or Inmates" (https://www.vera.org/news/words-matter-dont-call-people-felons-convicts-or-inmates) or Governor Kathy Hochul's 2022 measure ending the use of the word *inmate* in New York's law books (https://www.governor.ny.gov/news/governor-hochul-signs-legislative-package-promote-greater-fairness-and-restore-dignity-justice).

2. WorldPrisonBrief.com, accessed May 23, 2023.

CHAPTER 2: THE PALLADIUM

1. George James, "New York Killings Set a Record, While Other Crimes Fell in 1990," *New York Times*, April 23, 1991.

2. "NYPD Announces Citywide Crime Statistics for December 2022," January 5, 2023, https://www.nyc.gov/assets/nypd/downloads/pdf/analysis_and_planning/historical-crime-data/seven-major-felony-offenses-2000–2022.pdf.

3. David Gonzalez with Celia W. Dugger, "A Neighborhood Struggle with Despair," *New York Times*, November 5, 1991.

4. "CPI Inflation Calculator," US Bureau of Labor Statistics, accessed February 20, 2024, https://www.bls.gov/data/inflation_calculator.htm.

CHAPTER 3: DAVID LEMUS AND OLMEDO HIDALGO

1. To give some sense of the effect these arrests had on the Bronx: In 1991, there were eighty-three murders in Bobby's precinct. In 2001, there would be zero. Unpublished NYPD report: "Rico Cases 40PCT: Weed and Seed, 2001."

CHAPTER 4: BAD COP MOVIE

1. "The Psychological Phenomena That Can Lead to Wrongful Convictions," Innocence Project, November 18, 2019.

CHAPTER 6: NO RETREAT, NO SURRENDER

1. I reached out multiple times to Detectives Donnelly and Aiello back then, but both said their lawyers had advised them not to speak with me.

CHAPTER 8: THE HEARING

1. Benjamin Weiser, "Doubting Case, a Prosecutor Helped the Defense," *New York Times,* June 23, 2008.

CHAPTER 10: 74 MINUTES

1. Gary L. Wells, Margaret Bull Kovera, Amy Bradfield Douglas, Neil Brewer, Christian A. Meissner, and John T. Wixted, "Policy and Procedure Recommendations for the Collection and Preservation of Eyewitness Identification Evidence," *Law and Human Behavior* 44, no. 1 (2020): 3–36.

CHAPTER 11: SOME TYPE OF GAME

1. Multiple efforts were made to interview Eugene Hurley, Bonnie Sard, Cyrus Vance, and all other major players in these cases on the record. They have all been given the opportunity to comment. If there is no statement from them, it is because they have declined to speak with me. "I don't participate in these things," Eugene Hurley told me when I reached out for the final time, on February 17, 2023, to ask him about JJ's case.

2. "Informing Injustice: The Disturbing Use of Jailhouse Informants," Innocence Project, March 6, 2019.

3. Sophie Lebrecht, Lara J. Pierce, Michael J. Tarr, and James W. Tanaka, "Perceptual Other-Race Training Reduces Implicit Racial Bias," *PLoS ONE* 4, no. 1 (2009): e4215.

CHAPTER 12: THE CHALLENGE

1. Beth Schwartzapfel, "'Blindfold' Off: New York Overhauls Pretrial Evidence Rules," Marshall Project, April 1, 2019.

CHAPTER 13: BOB AND CELIA

1. National Research Council, *Identifying the Culprit: Assessing Eyewitness Identification* (Washington, DC: National Academies Press, 2014).

2. Joseph Goldstein, "Jailing the Wrong Man: Mug Shot Searches Persist in New York, Despite Serious Risks," *New York Times,* January 5, 2019.

CHAPTER 14: ERIC GLISSON AND THE BRONX SIX

1. Chris Smith, "How to Solve a Murder," *New York,* June 12, 1995.

CHAPTER 16: THE FAILURE OF THE CIU

1. In fairness to the DA, the office made it an issue that at one point I tagged along with Joe Dwyer, the private investigator hired by JJ's lawyers. He was later disgraced, arrested for buying information from law enforcement. But I distanced myself from him early, and never used him

in my work. And I asked to follow the prosecutors around too as they did their work, but they turned me down.

CHAPTER 18: THE TOURIST SUBWAY MURDER

1. "End Police Deception During Interrogations Nationwide," Innocence Project, retrieved October 3, 2023.

2. Gisli H. Gudjonsson, "The Science-Based Pathways to Understanding False Confessions and Wrongful Convictions," *Frontiers in Psychology* 12 (2021): 633936.

3. Stephanie Madon, Max Guyll, Kyle C. Scherr, Sarah Greathouse, and Gary L. Wells, "Temporal Discounting: The Differential Effect of Proximal and Distal Consequences on Confession Decisions," *Law and Human Behavior* 36, no. 1 (2011): 13–20.

4. "DNA Exonerations in the United States (1989–2020)," Innocence Project, accessed December 24, 2022, https://innocenceproject.org/dna-exonerations-in-the-united-states.

5. Lauren J. Grove and Jeff Kukucka, "Do Laypeople Recognize Youth as a Risk Factor for False Confession? A Test of the 'Common Sense' Hypothesis," *Psychiatry, Psychology and Law* 28, no. 2 (2020): 185–205.

6. Bill Hughes, "The Murder That Changed New York City," *City Limits*, October 26, 2010.

7. WNBC, "I dress for the muggers," aired September 10, 1990.

CHAPTER 19: 11/11

1. Anthony Petrosino, Carolyn Turpin-Petrosino, Meghan E. Hollis-Peel, Julia G. Lavenberg, and Alexis Stern, *Scared Straight and Other Juvenile Awareness Programs for Preventing Juvenile Delinquency*, Crime Prevention Research Review, no. 12 (Washington, DC: Office of Community Oriented Policing Services, 2014).

CHAPTER 20: THIRTEEN ALIBIS

1. National Research Council, *Identifying the Culprit: Assessing Eyewitness Identification* (Washington, DC: National Academies Press, 2014).

CHAPTER 22: "US" VS. "THEM"

1. "Cruel and Degrading: The Use of Dogs for Cell Extractions in U.S. Prisons," Human Rights Watch, October 9, 2006.

2. "Understanding and Overcoming the Collateral Consequences of Criminal Conviction," US Department of Justice, Office of Justice Programs, 2022.

3. Bryan Stevenson, *Just Mercy: A Story of Justice and Redemption* (New York: Spiegel and Grau, 2014), 17.

4. Rachel Elise Barkow, *Prisoners of Politics* (Cambridge, MA: Harvard University Press, 2019), 50.

5. Erica Bryant, "Why Punishing People in Jail and Prison Isn't Working," October 24, 2023, https://www.vera.org/news/why-punishing-people-in-jail-and-prison-isnt-working.

CHAPTER 23: "YOU'RE BEING TRANSFERRED"

1. "Joe Biden and JJ Velazquez Discuss Criminal Legal Reform," YouTube, posted by NowThis News on October 28, 2022, https://www.youtube.com/watch?v=mJ11x0M4NvQ.

2. Corey Kilgannon, "They Were Unjustly Imprisoned. Now, They're Profit Centers," *New York Times*, November 27, 2022.

CHAPTER 24: "WE RUINED THIS PERSON'S LIFE"

1. Somini Sengupta, "New Law Releases Juries in New York from Sequestering," *New York Times*, May 31, 2001.

2. Accessed from alvinbragg.com, December 6, 2022.

INDEX

ABOUT THE AUTHOR

Dan Slepian is a journalist at NBC News and a veteran producer of its signature newsmagazine, *Dateline*. For nearly three decades at NBC, Slepian has spearheaded dozens of documentaries and hidden-camera investigations, and he is known for his in-depth reporting about the criminal legal system and, specifically, wrongful convictions. He has received three Edward R. Murrow Awards, more than a dozen Emmy nominations, and has been recognized by multiple justice organizations across the country. Slepian was the host of *Letters from Sing Sing*, a podcast that hit #1 on Apple's top charts and was a finalist for the 2024 Pulitzer Prize in audio reporting.

Founded in 2017, Celadon Books, a division of Macmillan Publishers, publishes a highly curated list of twenty to twenty-five new titles a year. The list of both fiction and nonfiction is eclectic and focuses on publishing commercial and literary books and discovering and nurturing talent.